Penguin Handbooks
Mind Specials

KU-326-636

Parents and Mentally Handicapped Children

Charles Hannam has three children: David, Simon and Toby. David, the oldest, is a mongol. Charles Hannam and Pamela his wife live with the problem of mentally handicapped children in their own family. His main interests are children and their education: he has taught in secondary schools and is now a Senior Lecturer in Education at the University of Bristol School of Education. With Pat Smyth and Norman Stephenson he is the author of *Young Teachers and Reluctant Learners* (1971) and *The First Year of Teaching* (1976), both published in Penguin Education. His recent publications are *A Boy in Your Situation* (1977) and *Almost an Englishman* (1979).

MIND (National Association for Mental Health) is a charity concerned with the needs of the mentally ill and handicapped, and with the promotion of mental health. It draws attention to inadequacies in the health service and campaigns for better standards of care. It runs homes, schools and hostels as well as advisory services, courses, conferences and a public information department. It has over one hundred active local groups who are concerned with alleviating mental stress in the community.

MIND, 22 Harley Street, London W1N 2ED. Tel: 01-637 0741.

Charles Hannam

PARENTS AND MENTALLY HANDICAPPED CHILDREN

Second Edition

PENGUIN BOOKS
in association with MIND

Penguin Books Ltd,
Harmondsworth, Middlesex, England
Penguin Books, 625 Madison Avenue,
New York, New York 10022, U.S.A.
Penguin Books Australia Ltd,
Ringwood, Victoria, Australia
Penguin Books Canada Ltd, 2801 John Street,
Markham, Ontario, Canada L3R 1B4
Penguin Books (N.Z.) Ltd,
182–190 Wairau Road, Auckland 10,
New Zealand

First published 1975
Reprinted 1975
Second Edition published in Penguin Handbooks 1980

Made and printed in Great Britain by
Richard Clay (The Chaucer Press) Ltd, Bungay, Suffolk

CONTENTS

ACKNOWLEDGEMENTS

I am very grateful to the parents who allowed me to come to their homes and who gave me time for an interview. All names have been changed or omitted and home and family circumstances have been altered to avoid identification. All parents received a transcript of their interview and agreed to its publication.

In writing this book I have made selections, and the responsibility for them, as well as for their interpretation, is entirely mine. I would also like to stress that several of the experiences described took place over a wide geographical area and this is not the description of what happened in only one town or in one local authority.

For the second edition, I would like to thank Valerie Andrews and Janet Thompson who transcribed the tapes; Chris Jones and Colin Harvey who made help available to me at such short notice; the University of Bristol School of Education who gave me some money to finance the project; Julia Vellacott who helped me so much as my editor at Penguins; Morris Malin for his constructive comments; and, again, Pamela Hannam who has given a great deal of time to the production of this second edition.

A MEETING IS
CALLED...

'I have the greatest, yes, the greatest sympathy for the mentally handicapped . . .' – Local politician at a meeting called to discuss the opening of a minimum-support hostel for the mentally handicapped.

In recent years there has been a vast improvement in attitudes to mental handicap. It is discussed openly, the media have helped with well-informed programmes and there is an increasing number of books on the problem. There is much understanding and sympathy and it is generally agreed that our society must look after its mentally handicapped members. Nevertheless, there is another side: like death, old age or cancer, we don't really want to know. Had it not been for my son, David, I would probably have settled for making a small donation when a collection tin was rattled under my nose, and when the bus taking the children to the special school went by I would have looked the other way.

Hostels, which in many instances are a good and economical alternative to hospitalization, demonstrate the ambivalence felt by many people. 'Hostels are splendid – but please, please not in our neighbourhood.' In recent years, although we have been trying to allow some of our outcasts to return to a semblance of normal life, there have been many cases of the sort of opposition I describe here. This has been directed not just at hostels for the mentally handicapped and for alcoholics, but also at half-way houses for people who have suffered from mental illness and been discharged from hospital, and those for ex-prisoners. All these have been opposed and also courageously supported. I attended the meeting to discuss a minimum-support hostel for the mentally handicapped which I describe here and I suspect it is not untypical of the sort of reception other proposals receive.

We had not been invited to the meeting, but a yellow slip had been put through a number of letter-boxes:

There is to be a meeting to discuss the Area Health Authority's intention to use the former maternity home (opposite the independent girls' school) as a residential hostel for mentally handicapped adolescents of both sexes in the age range 14–30. The meeting will take place at 8 p.m. on 8 November. We feel sure you will have a view to express, and urge you to attend, since this is the purpose of the meeting.

The slip was unsigned and so we were not to know who 'we' were – perhaps that was reasonable in view of the uncertainty of style and the emotive content. 'Adolescents' – that is a good one to start the adrenalin flowing; '14–30', the dangerous years, surely; and then the crucial point, 'opposite the girls' school' – mentally handicapped opposite the school! Who had called this meeting? It was all very puzzling, but no one had dropped the slip through *our* letter-box. Was this meant to be tactful? After all, the Hannams – the ones with a mentally handicapped child, you know – would be embarrassed to have such a matter discussed. A friend phoned and asked if we knew that there was going to be 'a protest meeting against the decision to set up the hostel'.

When we arrived at the meeting there was already a large group waiting to be let in. It seemed to me there were two sets of signals: from friends who were pleased that we had come along and from others who knew us but avoided us. It was a bit like being avoided at a funeral, not exactly because people are against you but because they don't know what to say. There is an invisible barrier between the bereaved and the mourners. This is how we have been treated for years. The stigma of having a handicapped child produces a reserve in others; it is not meant to be unfriendly, it is embarrassment, a sense of inadequacy and possibly a fear of contamination which hold others back. I have felt the same thing when I have had to make a conscious effort to go up to a colleague and say how sorry I am about a death in his family.

The hall was quickly filled to capacity, there was much tension and signals of recognition across the room. The group seemed to be massed for battle – but battle against whom and to what end?

A team sat at the chairman's table: a consultant psychiatrist, the community physician, the area health director, an administrator and the nurse responsible for community hostels. The vicar took the chair. I already felt so angry that I knew I would not be able to make a constructive contribution. Nothing had been said yet, but I sensed righteous indignation camouflaged by good manners of the 'do you mind awfully getting out of the way' kind; there was much bonhomie, 'we are among our friends' greetings, and of course a good sprinkling of hats and tweed costumes. The vicar called us to order, competent but also nervous.

'I want to welcome you to this meeting. There will be opportunities for questions and for informal discussion after our speakers. Let me say that I would be failing in my duty as a Christian minister of the Church if I did not state clearly at the outset that I am happy the hostel is going to be set up here and that I am sure that many of us will be happy to welcome the young people who are coming to live there. First may I introduce the team who want to tell you what their plans are; this will then be followed by questions. If you want to ask a question, put up your hand and I will give you a number and then I will call each one of you in turn.' This was a good move. It controlled what might easily have turned into an angry shouting match and it could have been difficult to call to order some of the formidable folk sitting there. He had taken a great deal of wind out of the protest sentiments: the Church had indicated firmly that it was *for* the hostel and I suspect that a large number of the audience were churchgoers. This was going to make it a little bit difficult for them. The vicar added, 'I would like you to remember that there are parents in the audience who have handicapped children; please remember that.' Thank you, a kind thought for the stigmatized – don't hurt us in public, just forgather to reject our handicapped children, I thought bitterly.

The community hostels nurse began. 'Let me say that anyone can have a handicapped child, it can happen to any of us and it is no one's fault. We want to give these handicapped young people a chance to lead normal lives and to bring them back into the community. The Ministry of Health and the Minister have strongly supported the integration of the handicapped into the community rather than locking them away and forgetting all about them. . .'

I thought that was a good beginning but it would not sway the audience: the Minister of Health was a member of the Labour government of the time and a group like this one would feel that whatever he advocated must be bad.

He continued: 'They are human beings, just like you and me, and I would like to say that I resent having to stand up here and ask for them to come here; they have the right to live wherever they want, just like the rest of us . . .'

Cheers for him, I thought, but not a good move. 'The handicapped' – have they got rights? Should anyone be able to move where they like? Surely only if they can pay high prices for houses in the area, for that is how we exclude 'undesirables'. Students are bad enough, but at least there is a chance that they come from nice homes and will have 'careers' – I felt that a shudder went through the meeting at such offensive honesty and commitment to the rights of the handicapped. Not a good political move, but what a smashing bloke!

Next the consultant psychiatrist. A consultant and a psychiatrist, here was a concentration of authority which was hard to ignore. He was gentle, authoritative and lacking in any kind of arrogance. He was listened to with great attention. I looked round the hall and I knew so many people there, yet I couldn't tell what they were thinking. Was he making sense to them, I wondered? He told us that the people who were to come to the hostel would be suitable for a life outside hospital. At last, because of the enlightened policies of the Minister, money had been put aside for the less glamorous aspects of health care: provision for the old and the mentally handicapped. The authorities were trying to reduce the numbers in hospital because many people from these groups were living there but were not ill. Many suffered from what is now fashionably called Down's Syndrome. What, he asked, was wrong with the word 'mongol', with which everyone was familiar?* He did not know. They looked younger than their years, they lacked drive. He was certain there would be fears about sexual behaviour but there was in general a lack of sexual drive among such people. They were timid, they were not used to independence and this would be a first step towards teaching them to be self-reliant.

The vicar asked people to put up their hands if they wanted to ask questions and twelve numbers were allocated.

The second question was a friendly one. It was not really a question but a statement: 'We are pleased to have the mentally handicapped among us. This is an opportunity to help.' There was very little clapping from the rest of the audience. I felt a great pressure of anger rising in me. Where was the support?

The next question brought us right up against the real issues: 'I have the greatest sympathy, yes, the greatest sympathy with these unfortunate people' – I almost hoped he would say, 'Some of my best friends are mentally handicapped', but no

---

* Throughout this book I have used the description 'mongol' when talking about those with Down's Syndrome. I realize that there is a move to stop using this term, partly because it is not accurate and partly because of its racist implications. On the other hand the majority of people are familiar with the word 'mongol'. I tell others that my son is a mongol. If I said 'He is suffering from Down's Syndrome' I would feel as pretentious as if I had said that someone had 'passed away' rather than died. Changing names does not necessarily remove the problem.

such luck – 'that is not the issue, it is this: the hostel will be sited on one of the most dangerous traffic routes in the city and I am afraid there may be accidents. What plans are there to make sure this will not happen?'

It is true that cars rush down that road in the morning. Many times I have had to scuttle backwards and forwards as they race down the hill, bringing girls to school, causing congestion and sometimes accidents. But it had already been said that if the handicapped were to be introduced to living in hostels, coping with traffic would be an important skill to learn. My mentally handicapped son has learnt about the dangers of traffic – he stops by the roadside and waits – so it can be done. Yes, anxiety about traffic and worry about safety were good points. The hostel is made to seem completely unsuitable, though sympathy and concern have been expressed.

The next question came nearer the real issue: 'We are setting up a hostel opposite the girls' school. There is a traffic problem and we are worried about the safety of the girls. Can we be sure they are safe?'

There was a rustle of well-bred 'hear, hears', some clapping and murmurs of agreement. The undercurrent of the meeting was emerging. Here were parents worried that their daughters would be contaminated by the ugly, the ungainly and the helpless, or worse; because, on emotional occasions like this one, the distinction between mental illness and mental handicap is blurred, and an association between sexual offenders and the mentally handicapped was implied. Their daughters were at risk.

The psychiatrist replied that the aim of the project was to teach mentally handicapped people how to live in the community. There would be support and supervision and, from the criminal statistics, it was quite evident that the mentally handicapped did not make a significant contribution to the figures for crime.

No one seemed to have heard the reply. It was an interesting study in the dynamics of a large group massed for fight. Reason had very little impact.

The next questioner again had the greatest sympathy for these unfortunate people, indeed in his own family there was a child who had a handicap. This time there were two parts to the question: the smallness of the garden and the cost of conversion. Was it true that the cost was a quarter of a million pounds? Had the consultants been unanimous in their decision to site the hostel here? The reply was that there had to be a compromise. Ideally there could have been better sites but in the end they, all four people concerned, had agreed that this was the best choice.

This answer was accepted with an ironic smile. The questioner knew better but would not say more, implying that this had been a very odd decision but that the professional integrity of the psychiatrist could not be questioned.

Another question came from a working-class man with a nice local accent. How marvellous, a token worker who would show that this was not a battle for capitalist self-interest, because all classes were against the proposals. 'Sir, I have been a caretaker, I know all about these sort of people – they're all right when they're small but when they get older they get up to some pretty nasty tricks . . .' There was a heavy emphasis on 'nasty tricks' – it was implied that this was not just a question of vandalism, this was sexual activity, and an animated murmur went round the hall. At last it was coming into the open. The unbridled sexuality of the mentally handicapped, daughters facing dangers as yet undreamed of, the Mad Axeman and Jack the Ripper were about to be set on their daughters. Daughters who, incidentally, go into subnormality hospitals to help. The comments made by the panel had been inadequate; the school was at risk.

The psychiatrist was somewhat purple but controlled as he explained that the sexual drives of the mentally handicapped were not a problem. 'No one can give cast-iron guarantees of anyone's behaviour, but the staff selecting people for the hostel will certainly take the greatest care, particularly in view of the strong feelings expressed here. Social inadequacy is a problem: it is far more likely that the young people will be afraid of going out than that they will rush blindly into the traffic. Years of institutionalization leave their mark. Too many of these people have been locked up in hospitals for no very good reason except lack of community support. These are the *real* problems.'

I wished some heavenly computer would supply me with figures for sexual offences committed by caretakers. I knew I should not speak – 'No cause is lost until the archbishop supports it', as they say. If the reply to the sexual innuendo had satisfied the majority they certainly did not show it.

The headmistress of the girls' school had her turn next. She was quaking with controlled emotion, or possibly shyness, but her question made its point. She asked whether the authorities could guarantee that her girls would not come to any harm, for she had her responsibilities both to parents and governors.

Not an unreasonable question, I thought at first. After all, she had to show satisfactorily that she had taken all possible precautions. Then a doubt rose in my mind: could the question have been put differently? Couldn't she have said, 'I am delighted that the girls in my school will have the chance to meet people who are facing great difficulties. What can we do to help?' It would seem that she too was awaiting the coming of the hostel with dread instead of openly taking the chance to practise the charity and compassion that was no doubt the subject of many a morning hymn. Perhaps it was as well for her that the main body of the meeting was above middle age. The young seem to approach the problem of mental handicap with fewer hesitations than the elderly.

The psychiatrist said that his own children and those from a number of local schools regularly went to the subnormality hospitals under his care and he could not report any unpleasantness. On the contrary he would argue that the young had become more sensitive and concerned as a result of the contact.

Another thought: the school knew about the coming of the hostel. The Health Authority had written to the headmistress and the governors setting out the plans and intentions – now it was made to appear as if, by some sinister plot, the hostel had been sprung on an unsuspecting community.

Questions continued after the parent of a mentally handicapped child had made his statement: 'Anyone may have a handicapped child. If there is a handicapped child in the family it imposes enormous strains; if the community can help it will provide a great relief. What the parents fear more than anything is what may happen when they themselves grow old and die. A hostel like this would help to end that anxiety.'

More questions about the cost followed. The plea of the father had gone unremarked and so had the earlier comment that the garden was too small for such an important group. Now there was another undercurrent of supporting noises, murmurs that after all we were taxpayers and the health authorities were notorious squanderers of public money. What was the conversion of the building going to cost? Was it £250,000? No, only £60,000 or so. Did that include everything? No, there were some landlord's repair costs to come. Of course it was going to become another extravaganza, the Concorde of the mentally handicapped.

From cost we went on to noise, and then to television. Was that going to be left on all night? And what about parties? The community hostels nurse stressed that the same restraints which all good neighbours practise would be enforced. I thought ruefully of the discotheques around us in the summer.

Were the doors going to be locked? No, the doors would be closed at night, just like an ordinary home. This was to be more like a home than an institution. An incredulous response: They can go out at any time? Won't they be in great danger if they go out? The potential sex maniacs and attackers of girls were now seen as objects to be protected from all the threats of the real world. In other words, please keep them locked up and as far away from us as possible.

A dignified question from a severe-looking gentleman: 'Is it all a foregone conclusion?' Yes, the hostel would open in two months' time. A gasp of horror went round the room;

officialdom had tricked them, this was not an inquiry at all. Not that anyone had ever pretended it was, except by implication in the note which had been sent round. Nevertheless, the protest was never formalized – it had been stopped by two important factors, the vicar and the presence at the meeting of quite a strong group in favour of the hostel. The last questioner made that clear. He was fuming with anger.

'Never in my whole life have I had to listen to such hypocritical cant, you smug citizens in your well-protected environment, you haven't even the decency to admit that it's the mentally handicapped you object to – all that rubbish about safety, the girls, it's the rateable value of your houses, that's what worries you . . .'

The vicar interjected mildly, more in sorrow than in anger, 'I'm afraid this could be counter-productive . . .'

The report of the meeting in the local press was bland. The question posed by the headmistress was there. Someone had said that the mentally handicapped presented grave problems, and I had said that I was delighted the hostel would give some young people in hospitals the opportunity to get out and begin to lead almost normal lives. The press might have praised the health officials for their candour, their genuine attempts to allay fears and to allow themselves to be questioned freely. The vicar was not praised for his uncompromising support for the hostel. No evidence was cited in support of the fact that the value of adjoining properties would not decrease. It was not pointed out that the pressure taken off subnormality hospitals would enable them to concentrate on the potentially difficult patients, while the relatively normal ones would thrive in hostels.

In principle everyone is in favour of hostels. The problem is: Where are they to be? Local residents have often quashed an application to have a hostel in their own area. If the residents happen to be articulate, reasonably powerful and well organized, planning applications will be fought.

Obviously my account of the meeting is not an objective one.

I was as much an interested party as the gentleman next door who was worried about the noise or the size of the garden. Campaigns for the mentally handicapped have had some impact; there were expressions of concern and sympathy, and because of this the opposition movement did not gain overall control of the meeting. Instead they rationalized their concern into fears about traffic, cost and sexual deviance. The twists and turns of the discussion are worth reporting because I suspect there have been, and will be, many meetings like this one all over the country.

I would be delighted if my son could eventually live in a place like this hostel. Not that the subnormality hospital he lives in now is a bad place, but here he would not have to feel he has been 'put away', he would be less cut off. Hostels like this one must be made acceptable to the community. I was impressed with the health authorities' candour and courage. It can't have been easy for them to have been exposed to the collective anger of the residents. It would have been far easier to do the thing by stealth, particularly as the building was theirs to use as they thought best. Accountability is important, and I hope that there will be a meeting in a year's time to which everyone who has complaints or questions will be encouraged to come along. I hope the hostel will be an open place where people can ask questions, where they can be encouraged to help and where they will learn to understand some of the difficulties of the mentally handicapped. I think it will work; a lot of the anger and frustration will disappear and everyone will, in the end, wonder what all the fuss was about.

*

Some time after the meeting there was an announcement in the local paper: because of the high cost the project has been abandoned. The house will be sold.

INTRODUCTION TO
THE FIRST EDITION

Seven families (twelve people) took part in the interviews, which took place in their homes and were recorded and transcribed later. These transcripts are the basic material for this book. Each interview lasted for about an hour and with two exceptions this was the only time I met the families and the only time we discussed the problem of having a mentally handicapped child.

Four of the families volunteered to be interviewed as the result of an appeal through the training centre and the other three families were contacted as a result of the help given by one of the parents who runs a voluntary playgroup for mentally handicapped children.

In the first instance an approach was m de to a very restricted group of parents: those with a mongol child aged between seven and eight and who had a child at the same special school that my son attended. My assumption was that parents who had the same problem as I would be ready to meet me and we would work together on the basis that we were both facing similar situations. As only three parents out of a possible sample of seventeen were prepared to be interviewed it is clear that my initial assumptions were wrong. I do not find it easy to explain this reluctance to be interviewed: of course one does not wish to reactivate painful memories, nor is it easy to talk to a comparative stranger about one's personal life – and to have what one says tape-recorded to boot!

The three families who allowed me to talk to them as a

result of the appeal were middle class and each, in their own way, had coped with their problems rather well – perhaps it is easier to talk about difficulties of the past rather than those facing one immediately. One family who had, in the first instance, agreed to meet me, wrote wishing me luck with the project and then added that they thought that it could not possibly do any good and would prefer not to be interviewed. A family whom I contacted through friends agreed to be interviewed, then felt they could not face an outsider and agreed to answer questions into a tape-recorder without me being present; then I heard that the wife lost her voice when she tried to talk into the machine. In that situation I felt that no good would come if I continued to press for help when it could only be achieved at such personal pain.

It would seem that, for some at least, talking about their mentally handicapped child is difficult, particularly when the child is still very young. The volunteers I recorded had already in their own way come to terms with the problems but, even there, I found on several occasions that the interview began with a denial of difficulties; the parents put on their public face, as it were, and only as the interview went on were deeper feelings allowed to emerge. It was almost as if a second interview began when the tape-recorder was switched off! This is a phenomenon well known to all interviewers: one almost wished one had a second tape-recorder that could be switched on when the first went off and that the less controlled and un-rehearsed parts of the interview could be preserved. One husband of a family that was coping particularly well said, at the end of our interview, that when he had the news that the child was mentally handicapped he had broken down and wept like a child, although he thought himself to be 'usually the hard one in the family'. Again, while the interview contained the official version it was often the case that the emotional bits and grievances came out afterwards. Most people were a bit guarded about these feelings and this seems to me entirely understandable; why should they open up to an outsider? Though all assurances of anonymity were given and each family received a transcript of the interview, at the actual time it was felt better to be cautious and guarded. This is not to suggest that there is a vast subterranean area of grievance, but to say that, if there were ever a deeper or more extended inquiry in this field, more than one interview would be advisable.

People answer differently to those whom they consider 'authority' or 'them' than they do to a detached outsider. As the approach I had made to one group had come through the special school they may have identified me with 'authority' and were therefore reluctant to come forward and express deeper feelings or even to be interviewed at all. It was certainly noticeable that the group I interviewed as the result of the playgroup contact displayed more feelings of grievance and resentment. The sample is small, the class bias is strongly middle class, and I would therefore hesitate to be dogmatic about the evidence I have collected. However limited the scope of this inquiry may be, it should be realized that those who talked to me are deeply involved and what they have to say should be heard.

INTRODUCTION TO
THE SECOND EDITION

The first edition of this book ended when David and the majority of children whose parents I interviewed were eight years old. The age of our mongol children was therefore a point I and the other families had in common, but despite this I did not really want to know what lay ahead. Adolescence is not an easy time for any family but it is especially difficult for those with mentally handicapped children when statutory provision for schooling comes to an end. As they say in the States, 'It's another ball game'. The school will have provided relief between nine a.m. and four p.m. on weekdays, and this will no longer be available. Local authorities make great efforts to have training centres, workshops and hostels available but, even if there are places, a new group of officials has to be encountered, a new set of payments arranged; the attendance allowance comes to an end and new benefits must be claimed. More important, there are physical changes: the sometimes cuddly or helpless child can become a powerful adolescent and will soon be an adult. Sexual development is inevitable and adds another dimension to feelings and relationships. The ageing of the parents is another problem. The wear and tear on them has already been considerable and, as the child grows up, they are constantly reminded that there will be no diminishing of responsibility; they will have to go on coping for a very long time. In the following pages I describe my own feelings when David was admitted to a subnormality hospital; they are complex, but I and my family are lucky. In the first place we could see that the move had to be made; secondly, a place was actually offered.

Training centres

Reference is made in this book to training centres. This was their correct title at the time of some of the interviews but they are now known as special schools since responsibility for running them passed to the Department of Education and Science in Spring, 1971. Training centres are for adults (16+).

THE FAMILIES

Families interviewed for the first edition of this book (all names have been changed and I have also occasionally changed other details to make identification impossible):

Mr and Mrs Davis

They have one daughter at university and their mentally handicapped child, Christopher, is a mongol and is blind in one eye. Mr Davis is a successful businessman and they live in a very comfortable house.

Mr and Mrs Hopkins

They have three children. The eldest, John (eight-and-a-half), is a mongol and the other two were aged six and four at the time of the interview. Mr Hopkins is a teacher and Mrs Hopkins was a senior civil servant before she married. The family lives in a large Victorian house.

Mr and Mrs Jenkins

They have three children. The middle one is the mongol (aged seven), although rather more capable than the handicapped children described elsewhere in this book. He has an older sister and a new baby had just been born at the time of the interview. Mr Jenkins has a managerial position and they live in a bungalow on the outskirts of a large town.

Mr and Mrs Mercer

Their son, Philip, is a mongol and is the youngest of six children. The oldest of the children was taking his 'A' levels. Mr Mercer works in the engineering industry and the family lives in a pleasant suburb.

Mr and Mrs Peters

At the time of the interview Mr Peters, a skilled craftsman, was out of work because of an accident and his wife had just broken her arm. They have two children and the second one, Mary (five), has a brain injury. The family lives in a council house.

Mr and Mrs Richards

Mr Richards was in hospital with a 'mental breakdown' at the time of the interview. They have five children, the youngest of whom (aged five) has a brain injury. An older daughter, aged sixteen, who works in a store, was present at the interview. The family lives in a council house.

Mr and Mrs Shepherd

They have two children and the second one, Stephen (seven), is a mongol. The older child, Joyce (nine), goes to junior school. Mr Shepherd is an accountant and the family lives in a bungalow outside town.

Mr and Mrs Williams

They have three children: Glynn is nine-and-a-half, Bobby eight, and Harold three-and-a-half. Bobby is possibly autistic. They live in a council house and at the time of the interview Mr Williams was unemployed.

Except for Mr and Mrs Davis I saw a completely new set of parents when putting together this second edition. I chose Mr and Mrs Davis for the first interview because we had come to know each other over the years, had met on various committees and school functions and I knew that their son had been admitted to the same hospital as my son. After that I decided to find another group of families. I tried to find parents with children who were adolescent or adult and had handicaps other than Down's Syndrome. It had struck me during the first interviews that parents with handicapped children who looked 'normal' at first sight had even more complex difficulties than we did.

I have again changed names and circumstances where they would lead to obvious identification, but in fact several of the parents said: 'No need to change our names; if we have something to say we aren't afraid of it coming out in public.'

Mr and Mrs Armitage

Their mentally handicapped son was brain-damaged at birth. He goes to a boarding school but comes home for the holidays. The parents pay for his school. There is a daughter who has left home. The son, Rory, (seventeen), looks quite normal at first sight. He came in and out of the room several times during the interview, and one of the parents would rush out from time to time to see what he was up to: he was stripping wallpaper from a wall in another room. Mr Armitage has a business of his own, is comfortably off and the family lives in a very well-furnished bungalow.

Mr and Mrs Danby

They are over seventy years old. Mr Danby has retired from work and has recently suffered a heart attack. Their only child,

Roy (twenty-eight), is a mongol. He was present during the interview and occasionally picked up phrases in the conversation which he would repeat competently. The Danbys were married for seventeen years before Roy was born. They live in a comfortably furnished flat on a local housing estate.

Mr and Mrs Davis

They had been interviewed before. By now Mr Davis had retired from his business before he had to; he felt that the strain of running the firm and having his son at home had become just too much. Christopher (now seventeen) had been admitted to one of the local subnormality hospitals. Mr Davis now proposed to devote as much time and energy as he could spare to fight for the rights of the mentally handicapped.

Mr and Mrs Gage

They have a mentally handicapped daughter, Stephanie (seventeen), who goes to the nearby training centre every weekday. There are two other children, one younger and one older. Stephanie suffers from brain damage. She looks almost normal at first sight, talks quite fluently and brought me her tape-recorder several times during the interview. The Gage family lives in a well-furnished and comfortable council house on a local housing estate. Mr Gage is a skilled craftsman and his wife works as a cleaner.

Mr and Mrs Howard

They have a daughter, Denise (eighteen). She was seen to be mentally handicapped from early childhood onwards although the cause of the handicap was not clearly established. Denise has to take drugs to prevent her having fits. She goes to a training centre. There is an older daughter who goes out to work and Mr Howard works in an office. The family lives in a house on the outskirts of the town and there is a large garden.

Mr and Mrs Strachey

They live in a suburb and have two children. Their older boy, Clive (eighteen), is brain-damaged but looks quite normal. He now goes to a training centre. Mr Strachey works for a bank; their comfortable house reflected prosperity.

Mr and Mrs Taylor

Their mentally handicapped girl, Jane (sixteen), has brain damage and is severely disturbed. She was present during the interview and at times made conversation almost impossible by her shouting, clapping and banging her knees together with a noise that resembled the slapping of hands. There is a younger son of twelve who was adopted by Mr and Mrs Taylor. Jane is at a boarding school for nine months of the year and this was the holiday period. Mr Taylor is a skilled technician. He has become self-employed so that he does not have to be away from home at the times which a regular job would demand and can help his wife look after the children. The family had recently moved into an old house which they were planning to renovate. Jane is now in a subnormality hospital (1979).

1 A PERSONAL STORY

I was told within minutes of the birth of my first child that he was a mongol. The young doctor made a genuine and honest attempt to deal with the problem; what he actually said was, 'I can tell you because you are intelligent'; it must have seemed to him that intelligence is good protection in the case of news of a disaster. But what should the poor man have said? I can't find a good formula even ten years later. I suppose that bad news is bound to be a shock even if it is broken tactfully and gently; when I was told I rushed to the library and looked for some guidance. The symptoms were all shown, but I was not reassured by pictures of hanging tongues furrowed the wrong way across, strange slit eyes, hanging bellies to illustrate a lack of muscular tone, and cross-sections of brain cells. I wanted to pour out my fears and apprehensions and I wanted to know too much at the same time. The symptoms were all outlined clearly enough; what was lacking was any information about what it would be like for me and my wife. What did we have to face, and who would help us? Could we take the strain? Why had it happened, and to us? Was there possibly a cure?

I remember a kind of roar in my head, a hot, flushed feeling reminiscent of when I was a child and had done something terribly wrong. I became very active, I saw good friends, I phoned around, but I can no longer remember what any of them said, although they were all most understanding people. They tried to give me advice and comfort, but I found it difficult to listen to them because I was in a state of heightened apprehension and could not cope with all the facts for some time. Even if I had been told adequately what was in store for me I still would not have found the information useful. All I knew was that there had been a disaster. Gradually I sorted things out: there was no cure, the disaster did not imply that we had done anything immoral, there was not necessarily any abnormality in us, there was no blame in the moral or biblical sense.

It was a great help to me to know that nothing we had done or not done could possibly have made any difference. The feeling of guilt was at first almost unbearable. I felt an almost Old Testament sense of having somehow done wrong and that this was a punishment. We had married when we were more than thirty-five years old, we had wanted to have a child, so there was no question of having made a 'mistake' and then pretending that it was all intentional. It seemed to me that in that case we 'deserved' a perfect child and if it was not, there must be a reason for it. I am an ambitious person, more competitive than I care to admit, and I value my own successes however moderate they seem to outsiders. Having a mentally handicapped child made me feel that I had failed. Somehow the earliest bits of morality welled up: I should have tried harder, this was not good enough. A friend arranged that I should see a psychiatrist and I talked to him before I tried to tell my wife that the child was abnormal. At that time I must have projected some of my fears on to my wife. Perhaps when I asked 'Will it drive her to breaking point?' I was really asking 'Have I reached my breaking point?' The psychiatrist was calm and sympathetic and I regained enough control to listen. I heard that the child would make progress, however slow it might be. The child would have a personality and would be educable in a limited sort of way.

Most important for me was that at last I could express my feelings of guilt, resentment and disappointment. Increasingly I thought that I must kill this child. This seemed to be a simple solution and all our troubles would be over. I was quite cool about this at first; I had to be alone with him and then I could do it. Before I went to see my wife that evening, I asked to see

him and the sister wheeled him to me in his cot. I could see
the signs of mongolism clearly, the shape of his eyes, the tongue
that was hanging out. I had been present at his birth – a
tremendous experience – and, without knowing it then, I had
diagnosed his mongolism. I remember going over to him and
seeing a tube in his mouth to drain away the saliva. When his
nurse took the tube out, his tongue was hanging out, and I
called out to my wife, 'Look, he is sticking his tongue out
already'. I was terribly elated and excited at that time. We had
done it, a boy, immortality had been achieved! I thought him
rather ugly but then I had never seen a newly-born baby before
and they are supposed to be ugly. Now I wanted to kill him
and it was a very frightening thing even to think about. Here
was I devoting my life to the problems of educating children of
all abilities, having campaigned for the abolition of the death
penalty in the past, and the moment my own child did not come
up to my expectations I was ready to reject him and even
prepared to consider killing him. I believe that these feelings of
ambivalence are entirely natural but they are nevertheless
frightening and it is perhaps better to express them than have
them increasing the mounting feelings of guilt and inadequacy.
When I expressed these feelings to the psychiatrist he asked me
whether we had given him a name. When I told him we had
chosen David he said, 'You may be able to throw "it" out of
the window, but you can't do that with someone who is already
a person with a name.' I remember feeling relieved and more
secure after that interview: I had been able to listen to what had
been said.

Later in the evening I was able to tell my wife and this was
the greatest relief. She realized that something was terribly
wrong with the child but for some time did not completely
absorb what had happened. At the time when I told her about
the child she had a new perfume on and was happy and radiant,
having coped with the birth and having produced a child that
she had really wanted to have. Neither of us can bear that
perfume any more. If I smell it anywhere I am immediately
reminded of that time. After leaving the hospital our friends

rallied round, visited us and let us talk endlessly, but did not tell us what we ought to do. Sympathy by itself is useless. It is good to know that others feel for you, but it took me no further with my own need to deal with the shock. We made jokes to each other. It happened at Christmas and we made frivolous collage Christmas cards and sent them to all our friends. I remember being greatly amused that the only film on at the local cinema that week was 'The Mongols'. We needed a chance to express our outrage and resentment at the disaster and when we felt like that it was not much use pretending that everything was going to be easy and lovely. Some of the comfort we had offered to us is still good for a laugh: 'He will never grow up and leave you', the implication being that other 'nasty' children will persist in growing up and being people in their own right! Another crumb of comfort that was offered: 'Well, you didn't want your child to be a genius like Einstein, did you?' Equally unhelpful was the advice: 'You must remove the child from the family because the other children will imitate him and become abnormal.' That one came from a colleague, a highly educated and intelligent man; but these qualities do not guarantee sensitivity and I was really worried until the thought struck me that, after all, children do not become like the family pet cat either.

Any disaster that strikes will leave one exposed to the aggressive sympathy of the 'do-gooder'. The sort of people I have in mind here are those who come 'offering sympathy', probably in a similar way to those who drive their families to the scene of a crash. Another approach we experienced was 'What does it feel like to have a mentally handicapped child?', to which we longed to reply, 'We laughed all the way from the hospital.' Again there were those with strong religious convictions who came to help us with expressions of sympathy and spiritual comfort. To us they seemed to ooze patronizing self-indulgence. In other words, we were not easy people to help or support. Outwardly I put on what I hoped was a brave expression, wanting to show how well I was coping. Inwardly I was howling with rage and aggression.

Afterwards, in our own way, we had come to accept that David was going to be a mongol but there was still the problem of telling others – particularly the family. We decided to wait until there had been cell chromosome tests, when there would be absolute certainty. We really knew it was true, but we needed that sort of deadline. We reassured each other by saying, 'He does not really look like a mongol yet, let's take him up to mother's before it is obvious.' So we made our ceremonial visit with the new baby. Looking at photographs I took at the time it was quite obvious that he was a mongol and certainly not normal, but we all pretended that nothing was the matter. I waited until his tongue was in his mouth or until he opened his eyes wide before I took a picture and those were the ones that went to the family in the United States. It took us quite a long time to say to anyone, 'We have a child and he is a mongol.' It was particularly difficult to be polite to cheerful inquiries as to how the new baby was and to explain not only that he was well, but that he was abnormal. I talked to a teacher from a school for educationally subnormal children. 'What are mongols like to teach?' He said, 'Oh, you mean the ones with their tongues hanging out; no bloody use at all; we had one once but he was just a nuisance, kept on sticking his fingers into electric plug holes, had to get rid of him; they go to special schools usually, anyhow why are you so interested?' I was not able to tell him why and kept the conversation on an academic level.

The memory of David's early years is still something of a nightmare to me. Of course part of the difficulty was that we started having a family rather late and some of the things I found hard to tolerate were really due more to the fact that I had a child to live with and to adjust to, rather than to David's abnormality. In fact the first months were so normal that we began to have irrational hopes that the doctors might have been wrong or that we represented the exception to the rule. It was certainly not all misery and hell during the first twelve months or so; I can remember the delight I felt when he smiled and when he sat up for the first time. To encourage his powers of observation I fixed a mobile over his cot, we talked to him a lot and tried to stimulate him, and occasionally there were encouraging responses. I want to underline the fact that he is able to make progress, because when he was born I suspected this to be out of the question. As David was our first child we had very little idea of what was meant by 'normal' progress and we accepted the slowing up that came after the first year without undue distress, because we simply did not know what we were missing.

Having the next child was an important decision and we decided to go ahead after we had talked to a geneticist. Despite reassurances and the knowledge that 'lightning never strikes twice in the same place' (but statistically there is no reason why it should not!), waiting for the second child to be born was very disturbing and I found myself rehearsing comforting speeches to my wife in case everything should go wrong again. I was planning to kill the child if he turned out to be abnormal and had quite elaborate fantasies on how I would set about it. Much later I admitted this to my wife, and we found we had been rehearsing for possible disaster at the same time. She had similar fears, but we had not been able to admit these to each other. I was sleeping badly and tried to forget about the problem by working hard and investing more and more energy in it. It must have been infinitely harder for my wife. For me there was an abnormal child only when I came home in the evening and as time went on the stabbing realization of disappointment and resentment became less, but I still wonder what it must have been like to be with the 'failure' continuously. I can hardly describe the relief when the second child was found to be normal. I was there at the birth, and, the moment I saw his crumpled face with a huge nose in the middle, I knew that, whatever else, he was not a mongol, and he was so big and strong there was little doubt that he was going to be all right. Perhaps this birth, and that of the third boy who was also normal, did more good than any amount of counselling or social service provision. Failure to produce a normal child the first time meant that we felt that we would never be able to do it. This fear struck very deeply at our wish to be alive and to be sure of a kind of continuity. A child gives one a place in history and in time, and there is not much that can compensate if one loses out on that.

After our second and third sons were born the problems became administrative rather than emotional. All three children were bad at sleeping but the moment we asked for a tranquillizer for David our nights became less disturbed and, with better sleep, greater vitality also returned. I still wonder why we had to ask for the tranquillizer and why it was not suggested as a matter of course. We have felt all along that suggestions and help have not been forthcoming readily enough. It may well be still the same assumption ('because you are intelligent') that has made social workers steer clear of offering help. Perhaps we are so used to 'self-help' that it looks as if we have no problems, but I would ask all those who come into contact with families who have mentally handicapped children in them to probe carefully and see what the difficulties are.

The greatest help was the special school. It was suggested to us that we might try to get David in before he was five and we took him to see the principal. David immediately climbed on her desk and roared round the office; she understood straight away what it was like coping with him at home, and offered to take him. To have David away from home between nine and four was our greatest relief. We are sure that the school has helped him to become better able to live in the family. Over the years there has been real progress. It has been slow but suddenly we realize that he can do things that we never thought he would be able to do. He can now say a number of words. Perhaps the greatest breakthrough was when he learnt what 'Yes' meant. First he could nod in assent and now he actually says 'Yes'. This meant the end of constant temper tantrums due to frustration. How were we to guess that he wanted orange juice when we gave him toast? Then we would become angry because he just threw it all on the floor. Now he is ten and he can be much more co-operative, and this

35

makes a sort of benevolent circle – he is better tempered, so we become more tolerant; he is more affectionate, so we can return affection. There are still frightful messes. He can be dreadfully single-minded: if he wants to do something it is not easy to distract him or to stop him. He enjoys emptying buckets of water on to the pavement and after a time a situation develops that reminds us of the 'Sorcerer's Apprentice' – water everywhere. Then we have to be firm, that leads to a tantrum in turn, and then I become angry. I hate the thought of bringing up children to unquestioning obedience or squashing their initiative, but then I am always doing what conflicts with all our beliefs. At times I feel that I am very authoritarian with David. All the earlier fears and disappointments well up and I become uncontrollably angry with him. Last Christmas he climbed up to the top of the house and dropped our second son Simon's Lego engine right to the bottom. It exploded into all its component parts and was broken, fortunately not beyond repair. I rushed upstairs and slapped him so hard that my hand hurt. I then felt awful and wanted to make it up to him but I could not do it.

His relationship with his younger brothers is obviously complex; they are absolutely devoted to him although he spoils their games and he can hurt them. Perhaps he is an ideal brother: he is worse at everything they can do and he does not represent the challenge of an older 'superior' sibling. To our second boy, Simon, he gives security. He has said: 'I can't go to sleep without David, he protects me from nightmares.' On many mornings we have found one or other child in David's bed where they have crept for comfort. When the boys were very small I was always afraid that David might harm them and my wife thinks that these fears were quite realistic; she never felt able to leave him with another baby and even now he is quite capable of dangerous tricks. He thinks it is a huge joke to give a little push while someone is going down the stairs in front of him. But there are other times when he can be very funny and he amuses all of us when he dances or sings a nursery rhyme. He can paint in the manner of Jackson Pollock and lately has drawn figures that have faces and feet. He used to run away, which was of course dreadfully worrying, but now we can let him go into the square where he can sit for literally hours watching leaves fall or raindrops evaporate. Many neighbours accept him as an amusing oddity and in the house of friends he just walks in, helps himself to biscuits and turns on the record player!

Over the years David has become a very important member of the family. But we can't look after him for ever and his eventual removal will worry the other two. We can't take such a step lightly. Lately he has learnt to cope with going into temporary care in the residential unit: he comes home a bit restless but he is certainly not disturbed. This unit has enabled us to have holidays with the other two boys and this again has helped to lessen tension.

I have compiled this book because I feel that the needs of parents are not sufficiently understood. Time and time again the parents to whom I talked recounted difficulties like my own – they received no advice, or they would not hear it, and their burden of guilt was like my own. I marvel at the people who, when writing about their handicapped children, say they found help through their faith or their churches. No parent I interviewed mentioned this as a help but of course they may just have felt shy at mentioning such a thing at an interview. At a time when belonging to an official religious body and attending church is a minority activity it must be assumed that parents of mentally handicapped children will not have found any ready-made formula to see them through their troubles.

I hope some parents can use this inquiry as a point of reference at a time when they want more than anything else to be 'normal'. They can then perhaps see that they are not unique in their reactions and that the fears and resentments they feel are shared by other people. Professional help is essential at first. Being told of the disaster, however sympathetically, is not enough. I know that psychiatrists are in short supply but I am certain that my consultation with one was an important moment. Some people may feel that psychiatrists are only useful for neurotic or other mental disturbances. I am sure that if they were available during this time of great stress, when they know the child is mentally handicapped, and if skilled counselling were available while the child is growing up, much distress could be relieved. If professional social workers could be made more aware of the needs of parents and if local authorities would set up groups where parents could talk about the problem, the sense of isolation and feelings of guilt could be lessened and much suffering could be relieved. Nothing will make the child normal but parents can be helped to cope more adequately. A social worker with a heavy case-load might find it economical in time and energy to take groups of parents rather than individuals.

Both my wife and I feel this to be an important need but under present conditions it is not easy to help. It is difficult to take the initiative at a personal level. For example, my wife saw a lady with a mongol baby in a local supermarket. She wanted to talk to her, but felt reluctant to do so since it was just possible that the mother did not know there was anything wrong with the child. In any case it is not all that easy to approach strangers. She found out from the cashier in the supermarket who the lady was, and discovered that she knew her child was a mongol; so she spoke to her and told her about a local playgroup. No one in an official position had mentioned this playgroup to the mother. Such a playgroup is of immense importance. It is not just that there is somewhere safe for the children to play but that the mothers can talk together and exchange information.

If only we could persuade all authorities to recognize this need of parents, and to organize groups on professional lines, many of the burdens I have described could be shared.

When David was eight the future was still a vague thing. We were afraid of it, all right; we made some tentative inquiries about insurance schemes, applied to be put on the waiting-list of the Home Farm Trust and collected a prospectus from the Steiner Camphill Trust. The insurance scheme, although comforting at first thought, was not the answer: just to have someone look in on the boy after we were dead, send him the odd present and look after his interests in general was good, but it was all our futures we were concerned with, not just his. The Home Farm Trust seemed a splendid idea but inevitably the waiting-list was formidable and the entry requirements demanding. Would he be up to it? Looking through the form I almost expected to see that two 'O' levels would be required! The Steiner people sounded good – but the cost! Were we entitled to impoverish the family for the sake of the handicapped member? It was like the argument about paying for private health care, or education: both are facilities in short supply which can be bought on a black market at everyone else's expense. Our local authority would not pay, indeed why should it? It provided a very good school for the mentally handicapped; the bus called, fetched David and brought him back again and at sixteen there would be the possibility of a workshop or a training centre. The bus would continue to call for ever. No wonder that we did not spend all that much time thinking of David's future or, for that matter, our own. After all, the prospect of getting older is not enthralling: eyesight failing, hearing less acute, weight in need of watching; David's future was just another dimension which we preferred to shelve until we forced ourselves to be good and provident parents who gave thought to the years to come. In any case, David became easier to live with. He did not run away any longer, he walked with one quite well. He tolerated being away from home. He willingly, no, happily went on camping trips. A group of students took him camping for weekends and he came home contented, filthy and smelling of dirty feet and wood-smoke. The camp leaders liked him: 'He is less trouble than the so-called normal ones, I can tell you. He is a nice person. Do you know he sits there and watches the leaves fall from the trees and he is happy. No, he is no trouble at all.' I felt really proud of him; one thing was obvious, he could quite happily cope with being away from us and he was more independent than we had believed possible. For two years running I took him on a holiday in Cornwall which had been organized by the National Society for Mentally Handicapped Children. He obviously loved it, happily said 'holiday' after me and on the train he was no trouble at all. When we got to the farmhouse for his second visit, he rushed away from me up the stairs and he put his canvas bag on exactly the same bed he had occupied the year before. I found this a humbling experience: there were maps in his mind I had not given him any credit for. He remembered, he knew where he had been a year before; he remembered people who had been friendly to him. I learnt that mentally deficient does not mean the absence of memory or the capacity to enjoy. His world was a place and up to a point he knew his way, he knew pleasure and he knew where he was.

Over the years there was an improvement in his ability to communicate. Words were few but he knew more than he could actually say. Certainly he could name anything connected with his food. When I served him his plate of cornflakes he said 'milk' very clearly and then, as I was a bit slow, 'sugar'. When he responded like that we wondered if his speech could not have been considerably improved if a speech therapist had worked with him consistently, if we had kept up exercises and followed instructions with persistence and professional accuracy. David became more obedient. 'Don't run away' – and he would stay; he would take one's arm when crossing a busy road and his disobedience became more of a game. Like a three-year-old he would look at me wickedly when I said 'No more biscuits', and he would pretend to take one and chuckle happily at my mock indignation. He continued to find the greatest pleasure in his life in being in the square where we live.

His days were structured around the bus and so, of course, were ours. In the morning every weekday, except for holidays, the bus would come. One of us would have to wait for the bus and it could be late; one cold morning and it might not start, one child sick on the bus, or a traffic snarl-up, and there would be delays. As we observed wryly, the bus was never late coming back in the afternoon. However, he would tumble out and rush past me while I had a cheerful word with the bus lady and the driver. Always cheerful because here are the Hannams, the happy Hannams, the stiff-upper-lipped Hannams, 'Marvellous how you cope', 'We do admire how you are managing David' – to which I wanted to say, 'What sodding alternative have we got?', or even more ungraciously, 'Never mind the sympathy, how about taking him over for a fortnight?' In fact nine times out of ten it would be Pam who waited for the bus. When I did it there was a hearty display of welcome, 'Come on, David, out you come' as he clumsily stumbled to the door, a conspiratorial wink to the bus lady, cheerful thumbs-up to the driver and a wave to the other children in the bus whom we got to know so well over the years. David always seemed a bit cross when I received him. He was in a great hurry to get his 'dangle'. I am told that many mentally handicapped people love dangling objects in front of their eyes, or they tap, or they bang themselves rhythmically. David certainly became completely engrossed in this activity: he hummed, waved the rope attached to a coloured cylinder about and rushed around the garden backwards and forwards, almost as if he were receiving instructions from elsewhere. I hated this dangling activity; it was completely harmless but its very pointlessness underlined the limited range of his ability, a constant and painful reminder of the old pain and disappointment. His teachers would not let him dangle the rope either. Quite rightly, they argued that school was for work and dangling his rope was for home. We condoned the dangling because it would have been cruel to stop him and we

41

would have had to find alternative activities for him. As long as
he dangled he was happy. The alternative was eating or watching television. Had we followed a programme of development
there should have been planned activity: painting, speech
therapy, music, muscular exercises. The only problem was, of
course, how can one bring up two ordinary, very vital boys as
well, earn a living and run a large house? Nevertheless, my
reaction to dangling objects best sums up all the ambivalence
I felt during those years. The pleasure over small achievements
and the recognition of his development was one side of the
story, but the clumsy, monotonous tedium of his company was
the other.

We could never be at peace. Suddenly one of us would
startle the other: 'Go and see what he is doing', 'See if he's all
right, he sits on the cold stones for hours and he'll catch cold.'
David would stay in the square for hours, a permanent
spectator of other children at play, laughing as he watched
them but quite unable to join in. The children were never
afraid of him. 'Come and say hello to David.' 'Why does his
tongue hang out like that?' 'He's not like other children, you
see, he's mentally handicapped.' 'Is he all right?' 'Yes, it's
just, well, he can't do the sort of things you can, he is happiest
sitting and watching, and he goes to school.' Children accepted him very quickly. They never knew what to do with
him but, as far as I know, he was only teased once or twice and
then by a couple of boys who came from a home where they
were bullied by their own parents.

So David ran round the children, shaking his rope, humming
and looking up into the trees. It was best for him when the
blossoms came down at the end of spring; the thousands of
petals dropping gave him genuine pleasure and we would
sometimes throw a ball up into the branches to make more
petals come down. He used to sit by a railing to watch tiny
drops of water falling into the gutter where sparrows bathed in
the puddles. That and going to the zoo were his great joys.
There he would watch the giraffes for ages, would run on to
see the elephants and from there to look at the apes. I found

visiting the zoo an agony of boredom, particularly as I don't like zoos anyhow. We paid a succession of students, teenagers, anyone who was willing to take him and he went to the zoo with the greatest pleasure. He was at home in the house, he knew his way about, there was his chair in the kitchen, his place in front of the television set. He was firmly set in his routine. He would lean across to Pam and ask, 'Holiday?', and when it was Saturday and Sunday that was 'holiday' and he smiled happily. He went to school, possibly with resignation but certainly not unwillingly. Some of his teachers were enthusiastic about him; he was said to be 'a loner' but with a great sense of humour and very little trouble to anyone.

To some extent this was a time of reconciliation and acceptance. He was able to learn, he coped with the intricacies of living in a home and in a family, he was no longer naughty to a degree that had made our own lives seem chaotic and quite unlike anyone else's. David liked being in school, he could be away from home either in a camp or in a hostel without any apparent ill-effects – on the contrary, he seemed more self-assured and independent. As he was more co-operative he was also more accepted, and so he became less anxious and therefore less clumsy. From several of his teachers he received warmth and affection and he was able to learn from them. Paintings came home and also wooden constructions. When we saw the teachers they spoke well of him. The school continued to withhold information from us – 'We are always open, please call and we will be delighted to tell you how your child is getting on', and this was true; but systematic co-operation between home and school had not come our way.

I am describing the minutiae of living in the same house as David because they offer an insight into the lives of parents with mentally handicapped children. When there is a crisis or when parents are interviewed it may sometimes seem as if the families are living with a 'folk devil'. The disasters are remembered more clearly than the good bits of living together. If one has to make a case to social workers or psychiatrists the difficult aspects of life may well be stressed because help is needed. It seems wrong to talk about leaves falling from trees or sparrows in the gutter when asking for a place in a hostel or a subnormality hospital.

I am trying to sort out my own relationship with David. It was certainly never a good one, for he frequently bored me, disgusted me and even his harmless little tricks got on my nerves and could make me angry more quickly than I had believed possible. When I wanted to be affectionate with him he did not necessarily feel like being nice to me. Indeed why should he? Children do not exist just to gratify our emotional needs and yet they can do so, and in a happy family these feelings can occasionally coincide. There were moments of warmth. David shared a bedroom with our youngest son whose hand I used to hold before he went to sleep; suddenly David would stretch out his to me and I would sit there spreadeagled between the two, giving some sort of comfort before the terrors of sleeping and dreaming began for the youngest. With David it was the best sort of communication that was possible between us. Just as he remembered the room in the farmhouse he may also have remembered my anger and temper when he had been very small. It was easier when I looked after him on my own. Occasionally, he would tease me by not doing things immediately; he would look up, wait, and then pick up his towel or do whatever he was asked, but it took time. I could cope when I was feeling at ease but I would become sharp and impatient with him far too quickly.

When he was fifteen years and nine months old we took David to the local subnormality hospital. We had asked for his admission because it was the only solution we could think of. Pam had become ill. She had collapsed at breakfast two years before and we had seen a specialist. The social worker had come to see us and, after that, the hospital consultant. 'We will take him for three months and we can see how he gets on. We must do what is right for him, not just what is right for you or the family.'

I felt as if I had betrayed David but apart from the guilt

there was hope, the hope that he might go to the hospital and be looked after. I had asked myself several times: 'How much longer have we got? There will be other crises. Each time, David will be carted off somewhere else and we will just cope until the next thing goes wrong.' I had said bitterly to the consultant, 'What do I have to do to qualify for a place for my son?' Apparently my wife's collapse was not sufficient. 'Does a thrombosis qualify?' School was coming to an end, David was going to be sixteen in December. There was a place at the training centre and we had liked the look of it, but as far as our needs went that was not enough. The bus would still call at eight-thirty, and at four o'clock one of us would have to be there. For the rest of our lives there would be the heavy footsteps past us to the square, the biscuit tin and the dangling rope. I could at times feel tensions inside me which were unjust and irrational. The reasonable side of me would argue: He is your child, your first child, you believe in the rights of the handicapped and their essential humanity. Then there was the unloving, hating part of me which seemed to shout that without him all would be well. I wanted to shout at the consultant, 'I am sick of mental handicap and of the drag on my life. I am sick of sitting on committees, where we talk endlessly about mental handicap, the talks I give to sympathetic audiences, and the questions: "And how is David?", or worse, no questions, just non-committal discussions of the seasons and the unsaid part of the conversation: "We don't want to know, but we are curious, how are you coping, so your wife has collapsed, was it the strain, what a shame, you are coping wonderfully, we do admire the way you have brought him up!" I want to shriek (quietly of course) "Of course we have brought him up, what were we supposed to do?"...'

A few evenings ago I was thinking again that I could not stand his stupid face; thank God he was going into hospital for three months – if only they would keep him there for good. Then David held out his hand to me and we sat hand-in-hand and I realized that his face isn't stupid all the time, he can smile warmly and he only looks stupid when he is anxious, and

I often make him anxious. He could not say anything to me but I wondered if he wanted to communicate: 'Do not hate me so, I am your son, I can't help it, really I can't, I am here and I have a right to be here. I have no merit, my achievements are few and far between, I am clumsy, I spill things and I grind my teeth until you run away full of irritation, but I am your son.' I looked into his eyes (they are funny eyes, speckled round the iris, not just one colour but brown and blue), I squeezed his hand and I wanted to say to him:

'I am so sorry David, I don't want you, I have tried to be good but I haven't done very much for you. I have stayed away from home whenever I knew you would be about, I have looked after you because of Pam, not to help you. I try to sit as far away from you as possible at the dinner table, I snap at you when the sugar goes all over the place. You do all the things I hate so deeply in myself, my own ugliness, my clumsy movements. I want to be a jolly and humorous sort of man and you make me feel hateful, surgically cold and detached. I have thought about murdering you and you are my child. I watched you when you were born and I was overjoyed because you were alive and I wanted to have a child after all the murder and the death of the war. I wanted to shout at the world, "You couldn't kill us all, here is another one." You have made me into a hypocrite. Often when I have been "good" with you I have looked over my shoulder, somehow hoping that I was under observation and that merit would somewhere accrue because I was a good, jolly and tolerant father – instead I have felt that you were my own special little albatross, hanging round my neck for ever.'

We took him to the subnormality hospital a few days after that. I heard Pam explain to the charge nurse, 'He really is not much trouble, he can wash and dress himself and he takes himself to the toilet . . .' Lately that was not so, he had the most persistent diarrhoea and had been examined at the hospital. They had found nothing much wrong with him but our lives had become tense as we heard him constantly stumping up the stairs, I wondering whether it was 'my turn' to wash

his behind if it had become messy, or to clean up the seat –
hating every moment of it and knowing that it was not David's
fault.

The nurse in charge was obviously a kind, concerned man.
We were shown the hospital day-room and I was surprised
how pleasant it was, easy chairs, new carpeting and a television
set: 'Oh good, you've got a television set. He likes the television.' He likes the television! It was on at home from early
morning until the test card came on at night. If we let him he
would sit in front of the set at all hours and we let him because
we had neither the time nor sometimes the energy to do much
else for him. If I shouted at him and turned the set off he
seemed puzzled, made more anxious by my sudden anger and
irritation. The other two boys were not slow to move in on
that one, either: 'You've turned the set off, it's the only thing
he likes and you turn it off.' There is also a record player in
the day-room. We explained that David can put records on.
He used to squat in front of his player, turn down the volume
and put his head right against the loudspeaker. Sometimes I
would dance for him and that amused him, or I would pretend
to be King Kong and would beat my chest and roar – David
shrieked with pleasure and fear.

The nurse turned on the set especially for David. He had not
looked at me since we entered the hospital, and now he put
his arms round Pam. He was frightened, possibly because the
nurse wore a white coat and he had just been to hospital for
his investigation. Did he know that we were going to leave him
behind? I heard myself talking in my 'best' jolly voice: 'Oh yes,
he likes the television set', as if that set were going to solve all
our problems. David was pleased, though, and when he was
pleased he shook his hands as if they were wet and he was
shaking the water off. David looked out of the window at the
playing fields outside. The room seemed large and it was
well furnished. I added: 'When he needs to go to the toilet
he says "pee pee" and that means *both*.' Amusing, and helpful
too. Pam shouted at David, 'Goodbye, be a good boy.' She
always raises her voice when she talks to him; not that he is

47

deaf but she, and most people, speak to him a bit more loudly than they would do normally. I shout, and when I speak to him I sense an undertone of impatience and irritation in my voice. David did not even turn round, just waved his hand and looked out of the window.

We walked back to the car and when I had shut the door I cried. Pam lightly touched my shoulder and handed me a paper handkerchief. I have cried before, when David was born, but then I waited until I was alone in bed, and I cried when Pam suffered a collapse and was lying on the kitchen floor. Suddenly at breakfast two years before she had the most mysterious and terrifying convulsions, fell from her chair to the floor and I thought she was dead. Later, the consultant explained, 'It is not a disease, it is a symptom', and they looked with the scanner and their other equipment for the cause but they found nothing physical. Was it possible, I asked, that mental strain could bring about such a thing? Could having to live with a mentally handicapped boy for fifteen years, looking after him as well as the rest of the family, could this be a possible cause? It was agreed that stress might be the explanation and we then asked if David could be taken on by the hospital. A place was found for him provisionally and now here we were. When I should have heaved a sigh of relief I cried like a baby. I was determined that David should stay if they would have him; but it was the sadness of the situation that struck me so forcefully. What had we to show after fifteen years? Just a wave of the hand, David standing by the window, not caring all that much, it would seem. It would have been a thousand times worse if he had really minded.

It could well be argued that we had achieved something positive: he was now moving into adulthood and it was time to go. Many children leave their homes and it is after all a sign of maturity if that sort of break can be made. He has become an adult physically, and every year he seems to have grown farther apart from the family. The boys used to play with him; now they tend to ignore him (although they defend him to us when they feel he has not been treated properly), and in themselves they find it harder to include him in any part of their lives. David now needs to shave, his genitals are those of an adult and, although he has only a few words, his voice is a man's voice. He is over five feet tall and heavy. He walks with a heavy, clumsy tread and I can hear him clumping up the stairs, even his footsteps being a constant reminder of his presence. There is still the charm of his innocence. The most wicked thing he has ever done in recent years is to steal biscuits out of a jar in the kitchen or to help himself to a huge pile of sugar on his cornflakes. Even then he looks up and grins wickedly – for a few seconds I am able to respond, but deep down I have never been able to forgive him for the genetic confusion that produced him. The contradiction haunts me; here I am, advocating the rights of every human being, a belief in the educability of all and a dislike of elitism, but when put to the test I fail to cope adequately.

After three months at the hospital there was an assessment meeting and we were invited to it. We had been impressed with the standard of physical care David was receiving. He was certainly not unhappy there. It is a very open institution and that is important because it means we can visit at any time. There are no special hours, and therefore we know that a special display has not been put on for us and what we observe is what really goes on. The nurse in charge of David knows him well and all who work with him spoke warmly of his humour, his helpfulness and the fact that he was easy to look after. I was staggered – this boy whom I had almost dismissed as useless was helpful, he takes other men in his ward to the lavatory, helps them at the table, and is seen to be mature. Despite my rejection, my anguish, I have also had to admit that the move to the hospital was the right one for David. With us he led a static life, conscious no doubt of rejection and exclusion. What, after all, was his place in a family where we talk all the time, argue fiercely and do complex things like going to the theatre or to chamber music concerts? At last, among the blind the one-eyed man is king. In his ward there are men much more limited in their abilities than David and he has a place among them. The assessment meeting made this clear to me. We heaved a sigh of relief when they said he could stay with them, but we also had to admit that the right decision had been made for David's own sake.

I hope that this is a truthful evaluation of what has happened. Self-interest alone would have made me agree to his removal, but what is so important is that I can now come to terms with the fact that the decision was the best one for David. Not that doubts have not cropped up; there was the well-intentioned acquaintance who asked, 'Would you admit that David has been given a place because you are middle class and know all the right people? Would you agree that there are people who need a place at the hospital more than you do?' God save me from my radical friends with purer consciences than my own, but there is something in her question – all our lives we have derived advantages from the system because we are articulate, able to ask for our entitlements. We get the best out of the health service and the education system. Perhaps our lives will be improved because of David's place at the hospital. Who will define needs? Can I help David and the cause of the mentally handicapped by my awareness, my ability to write about the problem? Subnormality hospitals continue to have a bad press. The recent scandal at Normansfield has shown that only the involvement of the community and the brave independence of a teacher were able to end a dictatorial and monstrous regime. Our involvement with the hospital here will, I hope, be positive. When I tell people about the place they are curious and I urge them to come with me and visit David. 'You must see for yourself, it really is well run and comfortable.' Up to now few friends have come with us. But here we are. After sixteen years we can lead another sort of life. I have not forgotten the problems. I have talked to a group of parents and I hope I am able to state their case with more conviction because of my life with David.

2 HOW THE PARENTS WERE TOLD

My interviews show that in most cases telling the parents of their child's handicap was handled badly. But however well the telling is managed it is bound to be a great shock. As one mother said, 'I just sort of collapsed into tears, I couldn't make head or tail of anything.' When parents say they were told the news badly, they imply that they did not want to hear what they were told, and that they resented what they were forced to accept. There is no 'good' way of telling parents that their child is mentally handicapped, but there must be ways of not making a bad situation worse and of not adding to the suffering that is already bound to be considerable.

All the parents felt that they needed to have more than one meeting with whoever told them of the child's handicap. 'I think we were too shocked at the time ... anything else he said just went into one ear and out at the other.' If the parents do not have more than one meeting with the doctor, feelings of dissatisfaction will grow and misunderstanding will be inevitable. Those in authority who have to tell the parents will feel that the right thing has been done and the correct information has been given. Apart from feeling that something terrible has happened to their child the parents will be convinced that no one has told them anything and that no help whatsoever has been offered. There is a communication problem on two levels. The first is an educational problem: if a specialist is telling the parents, he may think that the information he has given them is clear and concise, but he may have assumed too much medical or general knowledge on the parents' part. It is not much use gently telling a mother that her child is a 'mongol' (or, perhaps worse, 'suffering from Down's Syndrome') if the term 'mongol' does not mean anything to her. As one mother said:

> My husband told me that the child was abnormal. This was a severe shock but since I knew nothing about mental handicap and had never even heard the name 'mongol' it did not really start to register for some time what the effects would be. I was naïve enough to think that perhaps some of the nurses did not know that the child was a 'mongol' and never spoke to them about it. Perhaps they were waiting for me to speak about it, and since I didn't, no help was really forthcoming. One of the sisters was quite good and helped a bit, especially with early feeding difficulties. Also the ward sister managed to empty the ward that I was in and left me on my own which was very nice: so I didn't have the constant nag of the other people in the ward with normal babies wanting to discuss and admire their own babies when I didn't feel like discussing and admiring mine . . .
>
> A specialist came to see John when he was about ten days old; she was very reassuring and very nice. I had been warned that she would probably be very brusque with the parents. I wouldn't dream of abandoning a child, but we were warned that she seemed to think that parents would abandon their handicapped babies at the drop of a hat and that she therefore had to impress on them that they should take their babies and how normally they could be treated and how normally they would behave.
>
> I think she underestimates parents to some extent, although obviously she is trying to do her best by the child. I don't think many parents would, if they were given a straight choice of leaving their baby in the hospital or taking it away with them, actually leave it, and if they felt so strongly that they were prepared to leave it, then it would probably be better both for the child and the parents if they were allowed to leave it than take it home and struggle with it. I think it is quite wrong that anybody should withhold this vital information, and I don't remember ever being told this. Although in fact both my husband and I were in such an emotional state that it is quite possible that we may have been told this and just not heard it.

Mrs Hopkins was treated with every possible sympathy but in

the last resort felt that, although everyone had been kind, no one had actually helped her. The specialist seemed to think that parents 'would abandon their babies at the drop of a hat'. Surely to help parents keep their babies they must be allowed to express their ambivalent feelings towards the child? The assumption behind the specialist's approach may have been not to tell the parents too soon because the shock might induce them to reject the child completely. A dilemma arises here; either one increases the parents' anxiety and self-doubt by not telling them anything or one bowls them over with immediate and brusque information and assumes that all will be sorted out by a competent social worker later. I wonder whether we are not dealing with the specialist's own need for a defence against pain and suffering here. The specialist had a strong moral conviction that babies should not be abandoned by their parents but this conviction overrode the need of the mother to work through rejection of the child to acceptance.

Even if the mother knows something about the child's particular handicap, doctors should not be blinded to the fact that this in no way lessens the shock. Indeed ignorance may be bliss and the mother who can immediately start to understand the complexity of the problem may be in a much deeper state of shock. As Mrs Mercer said:

[they] started to tell me all about it. Well, I suppose I made sort of intelligent noises because I did know what mongolism was. I knew vaguely about the extra chromosomes. I knew the outward signs; but of course when they left me I just broke down completely . . .

Secondly, the doctor may not be fully aware how much anxiety the parents are experiencing and how deep the shock may be; he simply may not realize that what he says is not heard and cannot be assimilated at that stage.

I felt unreal, that this could not be me, that if I switched off and went back to sleep, I would wake and find I had dreamed it. I even did not want to see my husband in a way, because that would have meant facing reality.

Anyone who feels anxious will be so controlled by these

feelings that the information which is supposed to comfort him will not register. This is a common problem in schools where teachers at first frighten the children in order to gain control, and are then surprised when the children won't learn anything even though they are quiet. The Jenkins are a case in point:

Mrs Jenkins Well they told us at the hospital . . . we went back when he was six weeks old, didn't we? We realized something was amiss, we hadn't any idea what it was and all they said was that he had mongol tendencies.

CLH Did you go together?

Mrs Jenkins Yes, together. He examined Peter at the time. I had never known anything like it; so I didn't know what to expect at all . . . I can't really remember; I think we were too shocked at the time that anything else he said just went into one ear and out the other.

Eventually parents will want to go over the bad news again and again and this requires patient and sympathetic listeners. There is no doubt that some people are 'naturals' when they talk to someone with a problem – so that a person feels he has been helped and that he has been understood. Empathy can be increased by training and this could form part of medical and social-work training. We found this quality among friends and with some doctors. This kind of sympathy must remain distinct from pity. When the parents sense that there is pity and, as they may unreasonably suspect, condescension, they will withdraw and become resentful.

One wonders whether the telling of the news should be left to doctors at all. Most medical students are not sufficiently prepared for the fact that they will have to communicate bad news. Their course takes place during a time of their lives when they are acquiring emotional maturity and working through their own problems. The aspiring doctor is so busy accumulating factual information and mechanical skills that he has little time for the psychological aspects of medicine.

Perhaps training should include simulation exercises based on the sort of material presented here. Role-playing may increase the student's perception of what is happening to the parent by increasing his self-knowledge and sensitivity. To be able to examine and experience the defences against painful reality may also give doctors some clue as to why they handle the parents of mentally handicapped children in the way they do. It is important that the parents do not lose faith in the medical profession or at a later stage they will not seek as much help for themselves or the child as they might, and may remain unable to hear and understand what the doctor has to say to them.

Mary is now four; she had her first serious fit when she was two, and was rushed to the doctor who told the parents to give her an aspirin. Later a test was made and the parents were told that she had a normal brain and that there was nothing to worry about. As the development of speech was rather slow the parents become more and more worried and again consulted with doctors, but again they were told that there was nothing seriously wrong and that if they were worried about speech they should see a speech therapist.

Then Mary had a prolonged fit and was admitted to hospital. Mr and Mrs Peters were told together that the child was brain-damaged. It was mentioned that she might be no more than a 'cabbage' for the rest of her life. Mr Peters felt it was right that he had been told the worst immediately – it was a hard shock but he always wanted to know the worst straight away. For Mrs Peters it was a different matter. She had a nervous breakdown for the next six months, blamed herself for what had happened, and could not sleep at night because she was (and is) afraid that Mary would have a fit in her sleep. Mr Peters thought it was cruel the way his wife had been told.

No one will ever know whether Mrs Peters's nervous breakdown was entirely caused by the news that the child was mentally handicapped, but of the parents interviewed, two of the mothers said that they had had nervous breakdowns and one father's stay in a psychiatric ward was said to be because of the child. It would be rash on the basis of one interview with each family to suggest exactly what caused the mental illness of the parents but surely it is clear that the parents of mentally handicapped children are at considerable risk. The news tests their resilience and personality to the limit and the need for support should be recognized. Mr Peters saw himself as the 'male' and 'tough' member of the family and thought it was right that he had been told; Mrs Peters was cast in the weak and feminine role and was allowed at least the 'luxury' of breaking down. The man had to carry the burden; he then suffered a serious accident at work and has been ill for quite some time.

Like the Peters family, Mr and Mrs Richards suffered greatly because the child was brain-damaged. The father was still unable to accept the fact that he had a handicapped child and the family must have presented a grave problem to the visiting social worker. As the child was brain-damaged and not a mongol there was the additional problem that all this was not immediately apparent (although, in fact, Mrs Richards suspected immediately that something was wrong, without knowing exactly what it was). A mongol can be spotted straight away, but other defects take time, and the telling of it may then come as an even greater shock.

Mrs Richards She had enormous hands and feet and she had giantism, and then, you know, they couldn't tell us an awful lot. They said they didn't know themselves . . . The doctor delivered her and was there at the birth and signed both of us as fit and normal – the baby normal! She didn't seem to think there was anything wrong.

CLH When did your husband know that something was the matter? Did you talk to him straight away or did he notice?

Mrs Richards No, I don't think so. I think perhaps he did, but my husband was reluctant to accept it, you know, recognize it; in fact he hasn't accepted it yet, that's why he is in hospital now . . . a week after they told us, he went

down with pneumonia, his lung collapsed and he hasn't
worked since and they thought it was due to the shock.
He has gradually gone down and he is in a psychiatric
ward now . . . He does talk about it, but I don't think he
can quite accept it. He resents anyone telling him that
there is something wrong with Jill.

CLH Who told him?

Mrs Richards Well, health visitors and people like this. I dread
them coming to the house because it always ends up with
either the visitors just walking out in disgust or my
husband telling them to go out. It has caused quite a lot
of problems in the family . . .

One parent felt that the family's own doctor was the best
person to break the news. The doctor probably knows the
family better than anyone at the hospital and may be able to
judge more sensitively how to go about telling the parents.
However, it will not always be possible for the doctor to be
involved in this way.

Mrs Mercer again states all the dilemmas: should the parents
be told sooner or later? Separately or together? Should the
parents be told that they need not take the child home? Is this
an ethical or socially acceptable alternative?

Mrs Mercer When he was only three days old I suspected
there was something wrong with him. I could see that his
eyes were a bit funny and I kept asking people around me.
I asked a nurse in the hospital and that very evening I had
the paediatrician down and my first thought was: why
have they waited so long to tell me? The doctor and a
junior paediatrician came charging down to my bedside
after my husband had gone and started to tell me all
about it. Well I suppose I made sort of intelligent noises
. . . but of course when they left me I just broke down
completely . . . I was just wailing I think; eventually I
just sobbed that I wanted my husband, and he came
straight back. Of course the poor man couldn't under-

stand what it was all about, having left me fit, well and healthy. That's the only thing I have to criticize.

CLH You said earlier no one knows how to handle the telling of the news that something is wrong with the child.

Mrs Mercer I think the father should be there too. I think it's a little unfair to tell him by himself, and have him knowing, you know; it's an added strain having to keep something away from the wife if you think she is not fit to bear it.

CLH Would you be in favour of sooner rather than later?

Mrs Mercer Yes, although I've heard many people say that you would want the wife physically to get over the birth. My argument is that this news knocks you right back again anyway, you might as well have the two together and get them out of the way entirely. It's something you have got to learn to live with. I was told that there were three mongol children in the hospital perfectly fit and healthy, their parents just refused to have them at home, and none of them had been told until the child was getting on a bit, and she [the doctor] thought, she still does, that the longer you leave telling the parents the more likely it is that they will reject them.

CLH Was it ever indicated to you that you might, as an alternative, put this child into hospital straight away?

Mrs Mercer No, never. No one ever suggested that there was any alternative at all, and I certainly couldn't have walked away and left him in hospital.

Mrs Mercer's son was three days old when they told her that he was mentally handicapped. Clearly she was very upset by the news and would have welcomed her husband's support at that very difficult moment. In fact, her husband was sent for as she was so distraught. For only one partner to know about the handicap is obviously a great strain, whether it is the father or mother.

Many parents were critical of the type and amount of information they were given when news of their child's handicap was broken to them. I think it must be accepted that there will often be anger and resentment directed against the teller of the bad news because he will always be associated with it and may always remain a part of the angry feelings aroused at the time. If the doctor can accept these feelings without becoming resentful and punitive he may in time be able to work through them with the parents. If, on the other hand, the feelings of the parents remain too strong and hostile it may be necessary to change doctors and talk about the problem to someone else.

When faced with the task of telling parents that their child is handicapped the doctor may already suspect that the parents know something is wrong. This complicates the situation. One family I interviewed already knew that their child was a mongol before they were told; the wife had worked in a child-health department and could recognize her son's abnormality by his face. Other parents felt that something was 'not quite right' about their baby, sometimes without being able to pinpoint just what this was. This was the case with Mrs Mercer (see p. 57). However, some parents will realize that something is wrong but will not admit the fact, and try to convince themselves that they are worrying unnecessarily. Praising, or possibly overpraising, the baby's progress can raise false hopes, as Mrs Shepherd found (see p. 60).

The trouble with waiting until the parent asks is that by the time this happens the parents know already – or they have a fair degree of certainty. The parent often knows much more than he or she lets on and, in order to avoid a painful confrontation, both sides in the 'game' collude and pretend there is no problem. For the doctor this is the least painful approach, but it must be remembered that the parents have suffered agonies of doubt and uncertainty, often in complete isolation.

Mr and Mrs Shepherd waited six months before they were told their son was handicapped. During that time they suspected something was wrong but 'it was a case of, if no one puts it into words it can't happen'. They had broached the subject indirectly at the clinic after a couple of months, but in spite of voicing worries about feeding difficulties and general lack of progress, their son was six months old when they themselves asked if their little boy was a mongol . . . and were told that this was the case.

Mr Shepherd   We found that they left telling us much too long. A couple of months, three months, well fair enough, but when we started asking questions, once or twice she approached the doctor and said, you know, he isn't eating and he isn't doing this and he isn't sucking his bottle as well as he should, well then was the time that we should have been told, when we were inquiring and worrying that he wasn't progressing properly, and knowing too that my wife had been working with young children.

Mrs Shepherd   I think they probably tried to sound you out; I took him in when he was about three months and she was talking to him and holding him and his eyes were lighting up a little bit and she said, 'He is quite a bright boy for three months, isn't he?' Well now, instead of reacting as she hoped I would and saying 'Well now, I am rather worried', I clutched at that as a drowning man would at a straw and thought 'Thank God, there can't be anything wrong with him', and didn't say anything and just went home . . . I do think over this, if you have a good understanding doctor, I think he is the best person to tell you, really, but as I said, we only had a young inexperienced one, and were rather unlucky.

Some of the parents I interviewed had been told together about their child's handicap, while in other cases either the wife or the husband had been told alone, leaving them to break the news to their spouse.

Mr Davis was told his son was a mongol and advised not to tell his wife straight away; however, like many married couples he decided that it would be impossible to keep the news from her and so went and broke it to her that evening.

Mr Davis Well, first of all, very shortly after Christopher was born, the doctor at the nursing home called me into his room and told me that the sister in the hospital had an idea that Christopher would not be a normal child. My immediate reaction was: 'Well if he is going to be abnormal in any way, I hope he dies.' The doctor also told me that I had better not tell my wife at this stage; however, I went out of the room and straight in to see my wife and, as I believe married people do who live fairly happily together, she sort of read my face and said 'What's wrong?' and in spite of the doctor telling me not to tell her, I did.

Mrs Davis I had been to see Christopher and I took one look at him and I knew he was a mongol, I could just tell by the shape of his face. It was easier then, I was glad someone else had told my husband because I didn't want to have to.

Many, if not all the parents will wish at some time that the child had died. As most of us love life and feel strongly that it should be preserved at almost any cost, this is a shocking thought. Rather than make these feelings of guilt become unbearable and secret it is essential that they are allowed to come out and be accepted as natural. If the parent has wished the child dead it is no use going into pious sermons on the sanctity of life. It is better that these feelings of ambivalence are expressed rather than suppressed. Once they have been worked through it may be easier for the parents to accept the child for what he is.

Parents can work through these feelings, as Mr and Mrs Davis did:

We both hoped he would die because he was very, very ill, but they sort of fought tooth and nail to save him, and they did, and when he was over the bad bout we both said, 'If he is going to live let's take him home as quickly as possible and do what we can for him.'

It is not unusual for parents to have fantasies about murdering their handicapped child and it is important that these thoughts, which are very disturbing to the parents, are talked through, so that in talking about them feelings of guilt and shame may be relieved. It is rare for a parent to kill a handicapped child but many parents fear that they will do something violent to the child. If these fears can be expressed without moral censure the tension may lessen and the nagging wish to harm one's own child may be understood as a natural reaction which is common to most people and not the result of unique wickedness.

A moral approach to parents, telling them what they ought to feel and assuming that all children will automatically be loved, is unwise – it will only make them feel worse. They will no longer reveal their genuine feelings and they will avoid discussing the problem altogether. Obviously one would hope that eventually the child will come to be accepted, but not everyone can achieve this. As Mrs Richards said:

> My husband was very reluctant to accept it . . . to recognize it; he does talk about it, but I don't think he can quite accept it. He resents anyone telling him that there is something wrong with Jill.

Mrs Williams's boy is now eight and she is not at all clear what is the matter with him. She does not seem to have understood the methods of diagnosis or the results. Here is a clear example of almost total lack of communication between middle-class doctors, social workers and a working-class mother who is intelligent, but anxious and upset.

Mrs Williams I first noticed that he had fits when he was nine months old; we didn't have a doctor when we first moved out here. I took him to the casualty in the children's hospital. From then on he was up there, he had blood tests and everything, and when he was a year and three months he had his first double EEG; then, by the time he was two years of age, I knew then there was something wrong with him.

CLH Did somebody take you aside and tell you about this?

Mrs Williams No.

CLH How did you find out?

Mrs Williams This is just something that I found out for myself.

I have already mentioned how the anxiety of the parents and lack of experience or insensitivity on the part of the doctor can make communication between the two sides very difficult.

Although it is clear that not many parents reject their mentally handicapped child completely, one mother was particularly upset that she and her husband had not been told that they could leave the child at the hospital, should they feel unable to accept it and care for it. Clearly the doctor wants the best deal for the child, but this should not override consideration for the parents' needs and feelings: they should be treated as adults and allowed to see the alternatives. It is extremely important that the situation is outlined realistically and that the parents are told what can and what cannot be done for the child. It is unrealistic for the doctor to assume that all this will be done by the social worker. Feelings can't be split into departments: the doctor can't be the one who deals with 'facts' and the social worker the one who deals with 'feelings'.

A survey conducted in London in 1964, quoted in the introduction to Barbara Furneaux's *The Special Child*, stated that 'in many instances the communication of the discovery of mental defect was handled badly'. Sadly I found this still to be true. How, and at what stage, to tell the parents is one of the most difficult problems facing doctors. Some may feel that if parents are told too soon after the birth the shock will induce them to reject the child; others will feel that to wait, while the parents' anxiety and self-doubt pile up, is to make the task even more difficult and increases the chance of parental rejection. Whatever doctors decide to do they should be aware of their own defences, which may make them decide on a course that is easier for them to tolerate than one which just meets the needs of the parents.

COMMENTS AND RECOMMENDATIONS

1. It is the parents' right to know that the child is handicapped and they should be told by a competent person as soon as possible after the birth. Where the medical staff suspect that a handicap exists, the parents should be informed, whether or not they have asked. Bland reassurances do not convince an anxious parent. An honest assessment should be given, allowing time for the parents to absorb information and to understand it.

2. Medical students should have more extensive training in conveying bad news to their patients. This is part of treatment. From my interviews it seemed to many parents that doctors sometimes made incomprehensible statements and then withdrew from the scene. This may not have been what the doctors thought they were doing, but that was how it seemed to the parents. Most parents want an adult discussion and don't want 'things' to be decided for them behind their backs. However, it is important that doctors do not talk so 'technically' that parents do not understand the information being given.

3. Advice given should be repeated. It must not be assumed that one session with an articulate professional is enough. A sensitive and competent social worker should work with the family doctor, who is the best person to see that the family does not become isolated and the mother depressed. Advice given without making sure that it has been heard and assimilated is not very useful.

4. Parents will often say: 'no one ever tells us anything', 'no one understands'. These must be understood for

what they are: cries for help. When parents with a problem go to see a doctor, a specialist or anyone else, I would suggest they make a list of the things they want to discuss. Once in the consulting room, or at the wrong end of a big desk, it is very easy to forget what one really wanted to ask. Try and write down what the advice is. It is all too easy to come out emotionally exhausted and forget it.

5. Help must be given to parents from the moment that it is known that their child is mentally handicapped. Diagnosis may satisfy the doctor's needs but for the parents this is just the beginning. There should be help and advice for the parents on how to bring up their child and where they can obtain help. Parents should ask their G.P., health visitor or social worker. It seems extraordinary that there are parents unaware of what help is available when one looks at the number of professionals who come into contact with a family. With the consent of the doctor involved, the Down's Children Association (address on p. 172) supplies schedules on stimulation, feeding, diet and exercise.

   There are a few Parent Workshops for parents of children under sixteen, and their aims are:

   (a) to provide opportunities for parents to meet and discuss each other's problems;

   (b) to make professional advice available on physical, mental and social development;

   (c) to give guidance on how to manage behaviour problems;

   (d) to tell parents of agencies which can give support and advice. One excellent project has been developed at the Ely Hospital, Cardiff. It is called the Portage Project.

6. Parents, and that includes fathers, need advice on feeding, toilet-training and behaviour problems. Behaviour can be changed or modified (see Janet Carr's book, *Helping Your Handicapped Child*), but the problem needs to be identified and the right sequence of steps must be chosen;

then there must be a decision on priorities. Ask for the social worker at your local authority social services department.

7. Speech therapy: parents can be helped to teach their children how to speak and communicate. Some retardation may well be avoided if speech training is begun early enough. Sign language and gestures can be taught (*Makaton* is one of these systems). Your social worker, doctor or someone at the school should be able to put you in touch with a speech therapist.

3 THE EFFECT ON FAMILY LIFE

All families cope with disasters differently; there are the 'solids' who have resource enough in themselves to cope and who can fall back on other members of the family, whose relationships are lasting and cannot be disturbed; and there are the 'brittles', who are shattered and helpless and need much support from outside agencies. Probably we all fall between these two extremes. Because extended families are not as close as they used to be, and families tend to live apart, another source of support and help is lost.

Not that all mothers and mothers-in-law are an ideal source of help. Mr and Mrs Shepherd describe very vividly the unease the younger generation can feel when in contact with the older. The neighbours are often not all that much use and again one does not always want to go on asking for help. They can be relied on in an absolute emergency, as when Mrs Shepherd had to run to the doctor.

When there are small children as well as the mentally handi-capped child there is always the fear that this child will harm the others. Mrs Hopkins was in this quandary and she quite realistically feared for the safety of her children. The Shepherds explain one of the difficulties they have with babysitters. It is one thing to ask someone just to sit in, but quite another to expect them to deal with soiled bedding.

Mr Shepherd Fortunately in my job I don't have to bring work home with me, but now there is a five-day week . . .

no, I don't find any strain with him in relation to my job. We have just had our holiday; well we have solved that now, you see, with the hostel [the local special school has a residential unit attached to it]; this solves our holiday problem, we have always felt before we could never go away much apart from visiting relatives . . .

Mrs Shepherd My husband has mentioned relatives. We have found that this is getting very difficult now; it isn't quite so bad going to my husband's mother – she will give the children practically anything – but we went to my mother last August, and she was a bit fussy. We found it was very difficult right from the word go. With meals he tends to go all over the place and she insists that you have him right up to the table and it's very difficult, and in the end we found that the only way we could cope was for one of us to stay with him in the room all the time, so that if my husband wanted to leave the room he had to get me from somewhere to stay with Stephen. We didn't tell my parents this, obviously, because they would have been upset. They thought they were giving us a restful week but it wasn't really, you know.

Mr Shepherd I think our biggest problem is that we have nobody around in the family. All our neighbours are pretty good, they can do certain things . . .

Mrs Shepherd When you say they are pretty good, love, they aren't really; no one will actually have him. Our next-door neighbour will have him for half-an-hour while I run to the doctor's, and I mean run, but no, no one has ever . . . the doctor did give me a bottle of dope that we could give Stephen if we ever wanted anyone to babysit, and we do sometimes go to the pictures and we give him some of this medicine and then we just go to see the big film. We leave at about eight p.m. and come straight back. Once every two months at the most.

CLH What stops you from going out?

Mr Shepherd Really, it is getting someone to babysit. Most of our friends rely on youngsters, schoolchildren, and we don't honestly feel we can leave him.

Mrs Shepherd It isn't only that you see, he gets – he did go through a phase a lot where he persistently had his bowels open in the evening, or worse, he would start to half change himself and the bed would be in a mess and I loathe the idea of neighbours having to clean up after him because I don't like having to do it myself, now he is eight, and so I didn't ask ... but quite honestly we haven't had anyone to babysit at all, have we, the next-door neighbour or ...

CLH Does this mean you go out in turns?

Mrs Shepherd No, it means we just don't go out at all. We go out as a family at weekends, but in the week we stay at home; as I say once every couple of months ... After Stephen had his tonsils out, he couldn't go out. You see if Stephen can't go out then I am tied to the house completely, I mean I can't even go shopping.

Mr and Mrs Davis mention the feeling of tiredness, a point which in fact came up in every interview. This is not just the tiredness after a hard day's work, but a sense of total exhaustion and depression that comes of an accumulation of bad nights, irritation and 'just coping'. Not enough energy is left for going out in the evenings and getting away.

Mr Davis I think the strain is that I am managing a large organization; by the end of a week sometimes I am pretty weary mentally, and I feel sometimes Monday morning that the weekend has been a dead loss from my own selfish angle. That's because relationships in the house have been strained, perhaps because of a broken night's sleep, perhaps he has been naughty. At the same time it is a routine one gets very used to, and I kid myself that as I get older and have these [management] responsibilities I get a bit tougher mentally ... my wife and I do snap at each other occasionally. It's what we would do normally, but we have got a little accelerator in the house that causes provocations.

Mrs Davis I can always dig up a babysitter . . . but we both get physically very tired. I just can't be bothered.

CLH What about your family?

Mr Davis My mother is extremely fond of Christopher but she only comes once a year, perhaps for a long weekend . . .

Mrs Davis And she has become extremely interested in mentally handicapped children now. She takes a great interest and is very good with him.

Mr Davis At work I suppose all the senior people know that I have a mentally handicapped boy, but he is never referred to, that is except by my secretary who has been to the house and knows the circumstances.

Mrs Davis My parents are dead now, but my sisters are not really interested; they all live a long way away. One of my sisters came to stay last year and she was sympathetic and made a lot of inquiries. She thinks that Christopher ought to be taught to talk. I said people can't make them talk . . . She is concerned for him, but the rest of my sisters, I think they feel that they have their own families and problems. We were a big family.

As with any children, the main burden falls on the mothers. The fathers can at least get away to work, and by immersing themselves in it forget the problems at home for a while. For the mothers there is no escape unless outsiders come and help or the child can go to a residential unit occasionally. Now that training centres have become part of the education service, ordinary school holidays have been introduced. This puts an added burden on the family. Holidays are surely essential for the teachers and staff but the mentally handicapped child at home must make life very difficult for the parents. Playgroups and residential units are a great help in holidays and these are dealt with in later chapters.

The break in the routine caused by the holidays upsets the children and affects their sleeping, feeding and toilet-training.

The Effect on Family Life

Unless there is a babysitter, such 'normal' activities as shopping, hair-cutting for the other children and changing library books become so unpleasant a hazard that they are dropped as far as possible when the handicapped child is at home. The family's activities are geared to the handicapped child's capabilities. There is no choice about this and everyone else has to go to the wall.

COMMENTS AND RECOMMENDATIONS

1. A babyminding service for housebound parents, particularly mothers, is needed. Perhaps this could be part of the home-help organization. Part of the difficulty is the expense of having continually to find and use a minder for the most ordinary occasions. There are many places to which a mother cannot take her mentally handicapped child because of the disturbance he may create. For example: supermarkets, libraries, even a visit to the clinic with another child can be a severe trial; one has to be watchful all the time. Even housework becomes more difficult. For these reasons extra help is essential if the mother is to lead any sort of normal life.

2. Nursery groups. From birth onwards, and not just when the child has a statutory right to schooling at the age of five, there ought to be nursery groups which stimulate the child and help parents to meet and share problems. Your local school may run such groups. Some paediatricians run groups and so do social workers. In other areas of the country there is nothing. Ask your G.P., your social worker or the head teacher of the special school for information.

3. The present arrangement for opening and staffing schools for mentally handicapped children only partially meets the needs of the parents and children. If hospitals can stay open all the year round so can schools. Obviously the staff need adequate holidays so this would mean additional staff. One realizes that voluntary help has its limitations, but this seems a good opportunity to use it.

4. The attendance allowance should be paid to all parents of mentally handicapped children who live at home. This would enable parents to pay for help in the home, either for cleaning or to look after the handicapped child.

   Mobility allowance, compensation for vaccine damage, and, if the child also has physical handicaps, help with alterations to your house may be obtained in some cases (see p. 162).

5. Sleep is vital for the morale and well-being of the family. Every effort should be made to make sure that the family gets a good night's sleep, if necessary with the help of tranquillizing drugs.

6. If taking the child on holiday presents difficulties, a short period in a residential unit can give the parents a much-needed break.

7. Experiments have been carried out in the United States and in Britain to find foster parents for mentally handicapped children. Properly controlled, funded and supervised this could be a great help. It would be less traumatic (and cheaper) if the child could go to foster parents whom he already knows rather than be placed in an institution or a short-term hostel when there is an emergency in the family: for example if the mother or father is ill, another child is born, or there is some other family crisis.

8. Nevertheless, parents would be well advised to ask their social worker what arrangements exist for putting up the child if there is just such an emergency. Some hostels reserve beds for emergencies; there are short-stay hostels and sometimes beds in hospitals. It is best to know beforehand what can be done. Memory lets one down when there is an emergency to be lived through.

9. Being away from parents is part of the growing-up process and the child should be given more opportunities to do this as he or she gets older. It should never be left

to the last minute, for instance when the child has to be taken into care in an emergency.

10. Having a mentally handicapped child is difficult for *both* parents, but the mother is more often the one who is at home looking after the child. Generally women suffer more than men if for no other reason than that they have to be with the child while the husband is out. The sickness rate of women with handicapped children is significantly higher than that of mothers with normal children. Husbands should not only share the burden, they need to watch their wives carefully for signs of stress or depression. At the Baytree, Weston-super-Mare, fathers were provided with a special workshop when links were developed between home and school. Fathers may have different ideas on the upbringing of children and may unintentionally interfere, to the child's detriment, unless they are included in the behaviour modification schemes and speech therapy.

4 PARENTS
AND OTHER PEOPLE

Having a baby is usually an occasion for rejoicing and much public congratulation. The new baby is paraded in the pram, everyone likes to have a look and coo over it and the parents can glow with pleasure and satisfaction. All babies seem to be beautiful, at least to their mothers, and there is the feeling of having created something perfect, a sense of continuity and the belief that a bit of oneself will live on for the future.

There is of course another side to having babies: depression, anti-climax and loss of freedom, but these are not the aspects that come out in public. When the birth has gone badly and the child is mentally handicapped, this is a tremendous blow to the self-esteem of the parents; they feel that they have either failed or been singled out by fate. All the feelings of guilt and inadequacy are heightened, and there is a sense of 'failure' and a 'spoiled identity'.

Mrs Mercer is one such parent who expresses these feelings. She fears both rejection and sympathy. This makes it very difficult for other people to help, and very often the result is either too much sympathy or just a denial of any sort of problem. Mrs Mercer thinks she 'bored people to tears'; in fact just listening was probably the greatest help they were able to give her.

Mrs Mercer They came in to see the baby and each one that came in I said to them 'Do you know about him?' and all held out their arms and said 'Of course we do' and 'Let me hold him'. But I did find difficulty in going out, although I did ask a friend of mine who lived across the road to tell everybody that I knew, so that I didn't have that awful feeling of suddenly while I am out somebody haring over and saying 'How's the new baby', looking down and saying 'Ugh'. You know, she told everybody, but I couldn't face the thought of seeing people and this went on for about six weeks.

CLH   Were you afraid of sympathy?

Mrs Mercer   Yes. I'd get ready and I'd think, this is silly, and I'd put on my coat and my lipstick and then I'd get the baby in the pram, then I'd take my coat off and send the children down to the shops; and, as I say, my husband goes out for a drink every night, and the first time I plucked up courage to go with him, I could see Bill over by the bar, and I smiled, a sort of tentative smile, and I could see his face drop, and I could see the sympathy coming out. He started across the bar towards me and I had to hare out into the ladies and have a little weep, and my husband sent someone in to me. I plonked on lots of powder and said 'It's all right, but it's Bill', and my husband went back and had a word with Bill and said 'For God's sake don't say anything' and gave me a stiff whisky and I felt a lot better, but I think it's people's sympathy that I was afraid of meeting.

Well, all of my friends were willing to listen; I must have bored them to tears and I think if I hadn't been able to I'd have gone nuts, looking back . . . I remember the first party we went to after Philip was born. There were all these people I hadn't seen for a long time and I felt they all knew about Philip and they were all saying 'Have you heard about it, poor soul' and I stood there with a glass in my hand and my hand was shaking and then this silly woman came over and said, 'Are you feeling all right, my dear? You look pale and you're shaking', and I thought, you know, nobody understands how difficult it is to be normal.

Mr and Mrs Peters show that the brain-damaged child presents a particular problem, for it is not obvious just by looking at many to see that there is something wrong. After all, a mongol in most cases is very markedly a mongol and people will make allowances; but a child with a damaged brain will behave oddly, which makes it harder to bear: outsiders will not make immediate allowances for the strange behaviour of a child who looks so normal.

While outwardly there is nothing wrong with Mary ('she is a beautiful child'), her behaviour is difficult. She will do naughty things impulsively, and in shops and other places the parents have been told that what the child needs is a good smacking. Both parents have been very upset because there have been remarks like that in the shop on the corner and by neighbours. Mr Peters had to go and tell people about the brain-damage, and he has found that hard to do. It is even worse for Mrs Peters, who is terribly upset if the child's brain-damage is talked about. To her, it is particularly annoying when people on television, for the sake of a joke, call each other half-witted and feeble-minded.

Mrs Williams had difficulties with the neighbours and finds at times that she is put on the defensive, particularly by car-owners who are touchy about their property.

Mrs Williams But anyway, there's one chap down the road, he's got a mobile van and since he's been in the street it's absolute murder with him. 'Cos nobody must even look at his van. Well, Bobby got this habit of going and touching his mirrors; well, I think a few weeks back the man said Bobby was playing with an iron bar. All it was was just a little bar, and he came up and he played hell with me. And I wasn't even here when it happened. My husband was supposed to be looking after him.

On the other hand, other neighbours were understanding and helpful.

Mrs Williams Well, the holidays are the worst time. Bobby

77

will be out on the roads and he's up and down touching people's cars. He broke an aerial off a chap's car next door. He never came and said to me 'Here's the bill'; which was very nice of him. I had a marvellous neighbour. She used to take him off for the day for me, especially when I was going through what I call a 'really bad stage'.

CLH This was when the third boy was born, I expect.

Mrs Williams Yes, now this is what I call the really worst. I know I had bad times before but this was really the worst. Oh, my neighbour walked in here one day and I had Bobby by the throat; well I would have strangled him. And she said, 'Put his coat on and I'll take him out.' But if it hadn't been for that neighbour one of us would have been done in, either me or him.

CLH When he was small, what helped you, how did you get over the shock?

Mr Jenkins There's not much difference with Peter anyway. He is a high-grade mongol and we just treated him as normal ... I've got a picture of him here actually; it's not very noticeable now, being a mongol, he hasn't got distinct mongol features which helps.

CLH What about the family?

Mr Jenkins Well, they probably showed him a lot more affection.

CLH Did they help you with the problems?

Mr Jenkins Well, I don't think we showed that we had a problem to be quite honest ... We felt we were coping, but we didn't have anything to compare with, we just went along.

CLH What about neighbours?

Mr Jenkins I don't think a lot of people realized at the time.

Mrs Jenkins They probably did, but they didn't say anything to us.

Mr Jenkins People don't say anything about it, do they?

Mrs Jenkins No, they don't come right out and say it.

Mr Jenkins You don't really know what they are thinking, do you?

Mrs Jenkins Everyone was very kind actually.

CLH Would it have helped if someone had talked about it?

Mrs Jenkins I don't know, I couldn't bring myself to at that stage.

Mr Jenkins We find it easier to do it now ...

Mrs Shepherd describes herself as 'not very much stiff-upper-lip' and she seems to find it easy to help others to talk about the problem. Once it is clear that parents of mentally handicapped children can talk about their children others find it easier to take the cue and ask questions. Often there is a considerable reluctance to take an initiative because of the fear of hurting feelings.

There is a reverse side to the coin: some comfort offered is so tactless that one must suspect either deep ignorance or aggression. Both Mrs Hopkins and Mrs Shepherd have suffered because of such hurtful remarks. Mongols are not significantly more musicial or affectionate than other children, but they have been given these stereotyped virtues which are continually offered as some sort of comfort. Thanks to the efforts of the National Society for Mentally Handicapped Children and sympathetic treatment by the mass media, mental handicap is no longer felt to be a disgrace and it is talked about more openly. But it is clear from the interviews that parents felt themselves to be the objects of pity and tactless remarks, which probably reflect the helplessness that most outsiders feel when something has gone so terribly wrong.

Mrs Shepherd We are the sort of people who go out of their way to find out what is available. The health visitor called two or three times a year, but apart from my visit to the clinic we didn't have any help at all.

CLH How did you feel at that time?

Mrs Shepherd We are not very much stiff-upper-lip people; I found it easy right from the word go to talk about it to people. I talked to a lot of people about it, it's part of our everyday life, and I can't talk about my older little girl, so I talk about Stephen, you know. It's automatic.

CLH   How do they react?

Mrs Shepherd   Oh, most people are very kind actually.

Mr Shepherd   Kind, yes ... they overdo it sometimes. We found that some people knew before we did, and once they knew that we knew, as it were, they were quite willing to talk although we did have one or two peculiar comments from the older people.

Mrs Shepherd   I started having a cleaning woman in one day a week and she said to me the other day, 'My uncle's got a mongol child and he says they are just like little monkeys', and this sort of thing. She is really a very sweet person, and you know they don't mean anything by it. It is just to be passed over. Another tactless remark we had when I had a couple of miscarriages was 'What must be wrong with you that you keep on having all these things?' This is the kind of remark that hurts me; they are numerous, and I think it is best to disregard them.

Mrs Hopkins again underlines the difficulty in telling a parent the news that her child is a mongol: it took weeks for the news to sink in, and again she found sympathy useless. Her strength lay in the fact that her husband could support her and she knew that help was available if she asked for it. What social workers and administrators have to bear in mind is that not all families have either the physical or inner resources to cope, although most of the parents interviewed here had. The questions Mrs Hopkins wanted to ask came up gradually and each time had to be absorbed in turn. Right at the beginning this would have been useless, but I can imagine that a group of mothers who meet occasionally and who have available to them the services of someone who is not only well informed in matters concerning mentally handicapped children, but is skilled in counselling techniques, could do much to relieve pressure and allay at least some of the anxieties.

Mrs Hopkins   After we had been to the hospital to have blood tests and had them confirmed we knew that the child was a mongol and I really began to knuckle down to the fact that I would have to live with it. This news was brought to us just after Christmas; after that there was a very heavy snowfall and we were isolated for a long time. I didn't take the baby out, even to the clinic, and not many people came to see us, they left us alone, which is perhaps the best thing they could have done. I was quite incapable of coping with sympathy, I just wanted to be left on my own: such support as I wanted came from my husband and not from my friends, who, I am sure, would have come and helped if I had asked. When John was born we had a home help, sent by the local authority, who herself had a mongol sister. It was thought that she would be able to help us more than anyone else. In fact she got on our nerves by continually hanging over the cot and making remarks like 'Isn't he lovely, not like my sister Margaret, she's ugly'. We couldn't stand her and after a time asked her to leave. We had no other help from the local authority except for occasional visits from a health visitor. Really there wasn't much she could do except give a few words of encouragement and a little practical help.

Mrs Davis received great kindness and found that the health visitor was the greatest help. But in general, the parents feel that people 'don't seem to understand'. This feeling is so common to all of them that perhaps it needs an interpretation – it may not just mean that no one understands what the handicap is all about, but that the particular needs of the family are not understood. Inner feelings are not easy to communicate, particularly in a society like ours which still gives value to the 'stiff-upper-lip' and where tenderness can still be taboo, particularly to men.

Mrs Davis   My health visitor could not have been more helpful

81

– a very sympathetic person and very considerate of your feelings ... for instance I was going to take him to a clinic and she said 'I wouldn't do that', and I realized after that I would have been very upset seeing all the other babies and how they were getting on. You forget how a normal child develops (my daughter was fifteen when he was born) ... I knew that mongols don't really develop.

Mr Davis My wife is an ardent reader on any subject that interests her and she took the trouble, I know, to read many books on the subject of training and upbringing of that type of child, so that she was really confirming, stage by stage, how she should be treating the situation.

Mrs Davis I got worried that I would say things to my doctor and he would say wait, wait and see.

Mr Davis We got the impression that our doctor would prescribe for him, but he wouldn't go out of his way to meet our problems or advise us.

CLH Why was this?

Mr Davis I can't tell you, it was just a particular doctor's make-up – had children of his own, all perfectly healthy – quite a few children, so he knew all about children ... but he never asked us how ours was getting on or whether he was making any progress. Now we have moved we have changed our doctor and he seems more interested.

CLH Have you ever talked to people who really understood what it was all about?

Mrs Davis No, people don't seem to ... although this health visitor has been kindness itself to me ... she has given me practical help. She retired just before the summer and she came in every day in the holidays and collected Christopher. She did this every day. She wouldn't accept anything at all. She took him out in her car, to the seaside, swimming, and said 'You have a good rest' ... she has been a very kind person but I feel I can't ask her again, you can't impose on people.

Mr Davis Nobody is unsympathetic, but nobody understands ...

COMMENTS AND RECOMMENDATIONS

1. Take your child out as soon as you can so that friends and neighbours can see him, can accept him and can lose their fears of mental handicap. Other children should be encouraged to play with the child; they should have explained to them the nature of the handicap and what the child can and can't do.

   Mentally handicapped people arouse fears, and while the National Society for Mentally Handicapped Children has done much educational work to lessen these fears, each family has to educate its neighbours. For a family that is already under severe stress this is asking a lot, but it is easier to teach by example than just to talk about the problem in an abstract way.

2. A friend or a neighbour who takes the mentally handicapped child for a walk will do more good than one who offers sympathy or compliments the family on how well they are coping! Having the child out of the house, even for just an hour or so, will give the mother a chance to relax.

3. Unsympathetic neighbours considerably increase the stress in the family. If the child looks normal this seems to make matters worse, because critical comments will be made more readily. The parents will have to be all the more prepared to talk about their child's handicap.

4. It is important for parents to be able to talk to other people about their child, whether those people are relatives or outside the family. It is essential for parents to be able to express openly feelings of hostility or aggression towards the handicapped child. In schools

where there is a positive attitude towards parents, meetings are held where problems can be discussed and explored. If the groups are skilfully conducted parents will learn that they are not alone in their resentment of the child and in the misfortune of having to cope with all the difficulties. To some parents who have put on a cheerfull front it is a great relief to admit their 'bad' feelings.

5. Babysitters prepared to deal with all the possible disruptions of a handicapped child would free the parents to go out together occasionally. Try your local colleges, churches and special schools. Many try to help.

6. Help can be given with behaviour problems but in a one-to-one interview the parent may feel incompetent and at a disadvantage. What was probably sound advice may be recalled as 'obvious', 'patronizing' or 'superfluous'. The professionals who work with parents ought to bear this in mind. If the parent comes to them with a particular problem it may only be a way of presenting a number of complex feelings; on the other hand, removing one practical difficulty may begin a cycle of improvements. The trouble is that mental handicap is not like a headache, it won't go away with a couple of aspirins.

5 BROTHERS AND SISTERS

When we had our second child, who was normal, a well-meaning colleague warned me that we should have to be careful because she knew of a family where the other children had begun to behave like the abnormal child who had, therefore, been put into a home. I imagine that this piece of advice is about as valid as saying 'don't keep a dog because all your children will bark'; on the other hand, it strikes deep and adds to the apprehension and fears that abound. We have certainly watched our children very carefully, constantly looking for undue stresses and strains (and therefore probably creating them!).

Jill Ashley Miller wrote in *The Times* (11 October 1971) about the time she had to decide whether to keep her child at home or not: 'The wise paediatrician had said at the time of her birth [a mongol girl], "However hard it is, always put the normal children first".' I am sure this would be very good advice if one knew what was best for the 'normal' children and what was best for the family as a whole. For example, is it better to face up to the problem of having a mentally handicapped child together, as a family unit, or does one in a sense deny its existence by having it removed to a home?

What I have learnt is that however difficult the child is, he becomes an integral part of the family structure. To split this part off, to send him to an institution, would change the dynamics of that family's structure, and it is therefore not a step to be taken lightly. It does seem, from these interviews at least, that the position of the child in his family very much influences the kind of problems that will arise. Mrs Mercer's son Philip is the youngest of six children who accept him as their responsibility and do not like it if the parents suggest he goes into a residential unit.

Mrs Mercer He is the youngest of six children which I think makes it a lot easier. I have got my others who are normal, bright kids who give me the satisfaction of their intellectual achievements, and this one is really like having a friendly dog around the place. We pat him on the head and spoil him . . . In fact he doesn't talk; but I suppose we don't really stimulate him enough at home, we give in to him too easily, but it has its advantages from my point of view in that I am not so wrapped up in him.

CLH What about the rest of the family?

Mrs Mercer Oh, they have been awfully good about it. My eldest boy, he was eleven when Philip was born, and I made my husband tell the children before I came home. I knew very well I was going to be in tears and they would ask why, so I made him tell Richard first, and Richard sat and listened to him and then he said 'Can we keep him?' In fact they have been marvellous about him and so have their friends.

CLH How do they treat him?

Mrs Mercer Indulgently. The boy who is twelve now, he got to the model-making stage at the age of six and Philip would sometimes get in the way and then of course there would be a great hoo-ha about it, but they are very fond of him, very tolerant, and very forgiving; they all look after him, too. Everybody has got their eyes and ears open for doors and things like this. The girl who is next to him in age, she is particularly fond of him. They rush into each other's arms when they have been apart for a day.

CLH Have you sent Philip to the residential unit at the centre?

Mrs Mercer   No. Never. No. The main objection comes from
my children. There is a great cry of 'If he were normal
you wouldn't dream of doing that'. I suggested it when we
were going to my niece's twenty-first birthday party;
they said they could cope and I said 'No, I think I'll put
Philip into the residential unit.' 'Don't you dare,' they
said, 'he doesn't leave until we go to school, we can
wait for the bus. We are home before he comes home'
... We wouldn't dare put him in for a holiday because
they adore playing with him on the sands. Each year they
would say, 'I wonder if Philip will go in this time, shall
we try this with him, shall we try that with him?' We
got him in last year and couldn't get him out.

Jill Richards is the youngest of five children. She causes great
difficulties to her parents, and the next brother seems to suffer
because of her. In these situations it is not easy to distinguish
what degree of difficulty is created by the mental handicap and
what is inherent in the problems of that particular family. An
older sister, Sue, seems almost unaware of her sister's peculiar-
ities: aged sixteen, she was present at the interview.

Mrs Richards   You know, it has caused quite a lot of problems
in our family. I have a little boy, he is eight now. My
husband has no time for him at all because he is all Jill
now. He very seldom talks to Bill unless it's to tell him off,
and Jill, like most mentally retarded children, is very
affectionate, very loving, although in the next minute she
can be very spiteful. My husband expects Bill to accept all
this. Well you can't expect a normal healthy boy of eight
to take all this and have his hair pulled. So of course he
will give her one back, then my husband will have a go at
him, then I have a go at my husband and that's how it
goes on.

CLH   How do the older ones see it?

Mrs Richards   Well, naturally they spoil her as well, but they
haven't pushed out Bill either.

CLH Do they make it up to him a bit?

Mrs Richards Well they try, you know. I try to . . . there are some times I feel I could give him one when he is naughty or playing up, but I don't. I think, well, if Dad is always on to him Mum can't be. He has got to feel someone loves him and wants him. So it is creating problems all round. I don't think people realize the problems it creates.

CLH Do your children play with her?

Mrs Richards Oh, Bill plays with her, but he is the next one . . . Oh, yes, you know, she is good fun, she enjoys herself and runs round the table. No, she doesn't worry me, but I worry when the doctors say we might lose her when she is seven, you know, but apart from that, well, she is like a normal child really, you know, in conversation and that.

CLH How would you know that something is the matter?

Sue People say she is a bit blue, isn't she? Across her nose and that, and people can tell like that, but I can't, you know.

I asked my second boy, Simon, to dictate to me what he thought about David. David was nine years old at the time and Simon was seven-and-a-half. As far as I can tell Simon does not seem in any way deprived or held back because he has a mentally handicapped brother. He realizes that he has some responsibility for David. We sometimes fear that we ask him to do too much but Simon likes his responsibility: 'It is very difficult for Mummy and Daddy because they don't understand him'. I know what he means: we are often intolerant and angry and it may very well seem to him that we don't treat his brother very well. David in some ways is an ideal brother: he is not competitive and everything Simon does is bound to be better. I typed:

Simon My brother is mentally handicapped. It is very difficult to speak to him. I find it rather easy to understand what he is saying. I think that is because I used to sleep in the same room as him. He is nine now and it is very difficult to get him from place to place because he wants to see all the same things all the time, like raindrops: he sits on the pavement watching the drops. His favourite animals are horses, cows and sheep.

David is a very mischievous boy. His usual trick is trying to get the biscuits out of the tin on the shelf; another one is getting into my bed, he also jumps on me and fights. He likes banging on his drum and makes us all go mad. He had a guitar for his birthday and he plays that. It is very difficult for Mummy and Daddy because they don't understand him.

When we go on holiday without him I feel very sad because I miss his snoring which stops me from having bad dreams. There is only one other boy who can cope with him and that is Adam Steele. He is the son of a doctor. David is very fat because he eats lots of bread and butter and biscuits. I have known David longer and I like him a bit better than Toby [younger brother, aged four-and-a-half]. We have some people who help with taking David for walks and help us. They are very nice to David.

Mr and Mrs Davis's boy is eight and he has a sister who is fifteen years older. Having a mentally handicapped child in one's family must arouse some fears and there is still enough nonsense talked about 'bad blood' and inherited defects to warrant taking all this seriously and discussing it with a specialist. If the whole matter is ignored these secret fears become harmful.

CLH How old was your daughter when Christopher was born?

Mrs Davis Fifteen.

CLH How did she feel about it? Did she talk about it?

Mrs Davis Well, we didn't tell her, we were advised not to, and this was a big mistake. We did not really discuss it until he was over a year old.

Mr Davis Yes, her friends had said to her that they were sure he was mentally handicapped. I don't think they should ever advise you to keep your family in the dark.

CLH Who is 'they'?

Mrs Davis Oh, the hospital, they said 'don't tell her', you know. He looked quite a normal baby after he got over his severe illness when he was born. My daughter mentioned it to her doctor when she got married, and he said it was very unlikely that she would have a mentally handicapped child and she has a nice intelligent child now. We have talked more about it since she married. One little incident I remember about our daughter: I had to go home and tell her that her new brother was in an incubator and wasn't very well and might not live, and I said, 'I am not going to worry you with these problems, just carry on normally and come home and cook me something and get on with your schooling etc.', and she said, 'Any problem that's your problem is my problem, because after all he is my brother.'

Mrs Hopkins's mentally handicapped boy is the eldest of three boys. All three were born close together so she really had three babies to look after at the same time. When there is a crisis, like the measles epidemic she describes, the burden is even greater because the family with a handicapped child has 'less to spare': it lives nearer the edge of the volcano and the fear is that everything will just go to pieces.

Mrs Hopkins When the third child was born we had another screaming baby who kept us awake at night and I tended to reject the other two completely because I was so exhausted by feeding and coping with the new baby. I think John [the eldest child, who is a mongol] suffered most from this because by then Richard, the second baby, was nearly three and we could explain to him what was going on, but John still was not talking although he was physically very active ... When Jason [the third] was born John went into the residential unit and started measles while he was there. He had to go to hospital when Jason was only ten days old.

At the hospital John would not take the food they gave him because it was not the sort of food he was used to . . . I decided that the only thing to do was to spend most of the afternoon there and take food for John myself, and so I did this: feed Jason, take him out in his carry-cot in the back of the car, park him underneath Sister's window, take John his food, give it to him, take his nappies off and try to treat his very sore bottom, play with him and talk to him; while I was there perhaps go back and feed Jason in the car, and then come home and deal with Richard who by then also had measles!

. . . I had to stop going out with three children as it was not safe to leave a pram standing with a toddler sitting on it and a baby inside it while I ran after John.

John's brother says he is miserable if the family goes on holiday without John, but at eight he is old enough to realize the problems of caring for John in a strange house, especially as he knows that John does not like the unfamiliar and would behave even more oddly than he does at home. On the other hand, the family is incomplete without him.

In the case of Mrs Shepherd the mentally handicapped child is the younger of the two and the older one seems 'a little bit frightened'. It may be frightening to see a brother or a sister doing things that are known to be 'naughty'.

This poses a problem for parents. Two systems of justice have to be set up which leave room for manipulation and my children often instigate mischief which David (the handicapped one) carries out very happily.

CLH Do you find that you treat the children differently?
Mrs Shepherd Yes, I think we have to.
Mr Shepherd It does make problems . . . We try to make it up to Joyce to a certain extent. I think she suffers a bit be-

cause we have had difficulties in having children to come and play. Other children are a little bit frightened and of course her friends are quite young and Stephen is quite big. Joyce says 'Mummy, can we come in?' and I say 'Yes'; they go and play in a separate room. I don't make them play with Stephen.

CLH Does Joyce imitate him?

Mrs Shepherd No, she doesn't. If anything she tends to worry about it and she will rush around cleaning up after him and looking at me with one eye and hoping that I am not going to be too cross about it. She is very sensitive and I think it tends to make children far too responsible for their age, which is why I am a little easier on her in other ways.

The Peters family consists of two children; Brenda, the older one, aged seven, is made anxious by her sister, and the parents fear they may have neglected her. Parents have to devote their energies to 'keeping going' and the normal children may feel neglected, just because there isn't enough energy to go round. Brenda's parents feel they have so many problems of their own that they have not looked after her well enough. However, she has a very understanding teacher in the school who gives her special attention because she knows how difficult things are for the family. Brenda is made very anxious by the 'dreadful' things her sister does and keeps on saying, 'Mummy, look what Mary is doing.' On the other hand, Mrs Williams's eldest boy largely ignores his younger brother except at night when he cannot sleep because of the noise and general chaos that Bobby creates.

CLH Do you get a good night's sleep?

Mrs Williams Well, sometimes he's there, banging on the wall . . . he's not a very good sleeper. He's there banging on the wall or singing. I was going to apply for a three-bedroomed house and I thought, well, if I could get him a room on his own and then put a little – I know it's an awful thing to say – put a little lock or a bolt on his door, to make sure he stays in there, 'cos it's not fair on the other one.

CLH   Does he wake the other children?

Mrs Williams   Well, Harold's got to sleep in with us, but Glynn sleeps in with him and there's Glynn in there shouting 'Shut up, I want to get to sleep!' But the thing is, when they put you in those houses they never want to move you.

In the Jenkins family the mentally handicapped son is between an older sister and a newly-born baby brother. Again the parents seem to be able to take the handicap in their stride and want very much to treat the children as if there were no differences.

Mr Jenkins   Peter is not unmanageable and we find that we can treat him the same as his sister. I don't know whether people will take him the same as they take his sister ... he's no different.

Mrs Jenkins   We've never had to try. In fact they make a lot more fuss of him than they do the others really ... though he can be terrible at times, when you are shopping he loves you to chase him round the shop; on the whole he is well behaved.

COMMENTSANDRECOMMENDATIONS

1. If the advice is to keep the child in the family it must be seen to be best for all the family, not just the mentally handicapped child. At this point the financial resources and the amount of help available must be considered. If the advice is to put the child into an institution then the potentially frightening effect on brothers and sisters must be taken into account; it may seem to them that a member of the family can just be removed at will, or because he is 'naughty'.

2. Normal children are presented with a number of standards of behaviour, whether in school, church or in the homes of relatives and friends, on which they learn to model themselves. The mentally handicapped child introduces another dimension into the dynamics of the family. Most parents try very hard to improve the quality of the lives their children lead. The pressure the mentally handicapped child exerts on them reduces the possibility of achieving a higher standard or even maintaining a degree of stability. Children find it difficult to accept two standards of behaviour. If they are told it is naughty to do one thing, say, to burp loudly at mealtimes, and the mentally handicapped child is allowed to do this, the normal child may be puzzled and even frightened. It is best to discuss the handicap with the other children, to let them share the anxieties of the parents and the reasons for their different treatment. In that way the mentally handicapped child may be accepted more readily and cause fewer feelings of resentment and bitterness.

3. The mentally handicapped child presents a burden that

should not be put entirely on any one member of the family, particularly brothers or sisters. It is important that they are allowed to entertain friends separately, should they wish to do so.

4. Brothers and sisters may be under pressure that is not necessarily apparent to the parents. G.P.s, teachers and social workers should be alerted to the possibility of stress once they know that there is a mentally handicapped child in the family.

5. Some of the programmes, for example the Delgado method to help mentally handicapped children, are demanding and strenuous. It could easily happen that parents become so preoccupied with the 'method' that the normal children are neglected. All members of the family have some rights and under stress it is not easy to remember that.

6 UPBRINGING

Quite apart from crisis points such as the actual birth and the illnesses, there is the slow grind of bringing up the child. At times it is difficult to distinguish the problems of 'normal' child-rearing from those specifically related to mentally handicapped children. All children get on their parents' nerves, they all make messes and they all need and demand more attention than most adults can normally give them. The difference lies in the expectations: with a normal child the stages of development merge and pass and, however ghastly the mess, one knows that in due course toilet-training will be achieved, speech will come and the usual social skills will be acquired. The mentally handicapped child often moves ahead so slowly that one despairs of ever achieving the next stage. The parents interviewed show that progress, however slow, is possible.

Many of the parents mention the speech problem. Speech is so vital. We structure our experience through speech, learning becomes easier, emotion can be expressed through words, and frustration is reduced correspondingly. When the child is unable to speak, a number of problems arise. Some children at the time of the interview were unable to talk even though the maximum age was eight. However, there were children who were capable of some speech and this helped enormously; the child could make his wishes known and there was correspondingly less frustration.

Mr and Mrs Davis describe very vividly the everyday problems. Like several other parents they dispel the myth that all mongols are affectionate, lovable and cuddly – this may be the case in institutions, where mongols often seem to provide the 'stable' element. They also bring out the problem of annoying habits. As married couples know, we all have habits that can barely be tolerated by the other partner. What makes the 'annoying habit' of the mentally handicapped child worse is that it is a continuous reminder of the handicap; spitting, teeth-grinding or even dangling bits of string hark back to the early disappointments, and accentuate other difficulties such as lack of sleep and the fear that the child may run away or do some extensive mischief.

Mrs Davis They say mongols settle down very well and are very happy, but Christopher isn't, he is a very withdrawn child . . . he likes to be among people, but he doesn't like anyone to approach him – and he likes, for want of a better expression, proper things rather than toys; he likes, real motor-cars, he won't play with a toy motor-car.

Mr Davis He doesn't see as much as other children.

Mrs Davis You see, if you cuddle him he pushes you away but he still wants your attention, so it is not easy to have a relationship with him.

Mr Davis You mustn't force him to do anything, you must persuade him; I have never tried to the point of hurting, but a slap on his backside, if he is naughty, is in his view a bit of a joke, so there is no point in pursuing the matter. You have just got to try and explain what you are trying to do.

Mrs Davis You have more impression on him than I have because my voice doesn't impress him: his father's voice if he is annoyed is far more effective than mine.

CLH What sort of things does he do?

Mr Davis Nothing frightful; he has this habit of lying on his tummy at home and just rocking and perhaps doing a little spitting out of his mouth, more or less makes a tune like pppppppp, this sort of business, and we want him to sit properly and be active, because if he lies around, particularly at weekends, he is apt not to have a full night's sleep and we suffer.

Mrs Davis He plays the record-player; he can do it all now except unlatch the lid and lift it up when the record's ended. The other difficulty we have, of course, and I haven't mentioned it so far, is that he can't talk at all and therefore communication is really very difficult for anyone coming to the house because they can't really converse with him at all.

CLH When he does not get his way does he have tantrums?

Mrs Davis He has tantrums at the school because they make him do things, which is quite right. He needs discipline and he does not get it at home; I get it if I insist on him dressing himself; he raises Cain and I can't stand it so I give him a hand, which is wrong, I shouldn't do it.

CLH Does he tap or bang?

Mrs Davis Flicks.

Mr Davis Forefinger and thumb.

Mrs Davis The spoon, he is a dangler.

Mr Davis He is a dangler all right . . . we take all pieces of string and anything like that away from him immediately.

Mrs Davis I don't know if that is any good either really, but still . . .

Mr Davis He will still do it if he gets hold of anything that will in fact dangle, he just likes to see it, to and fro like a pendulum . . . We go up the wall sometimes with this spitting business . . . and what is more people will say to you, 'Well, you know, that's nothing', but after months and years of listening to it, it is a lot. He grinds his teeth.

Mrs Davis Within the house he is getting fed up with his record-player; now we can't find out what he would like to do next.

Mr Davis He won't watch TV.

Mrs Davis He won't look at a book.

Mr Davis He likes being taken out . . . he likes perhaps going to a playground, but there again he will leave your hand

and dash at the swing even if somebody is swinging there. One day he is going to get his face split open. Now that we are fifty we can't catch him up and this is terrifying. He was missing from home once, because he can open doors now, and my wife rang me up at work and said 'Christopher is missing'. I am in the middle of a meeting. I collected two of my staff and said 'We have to dash off home to do a search for Christopher', and by the time we had got there he had turned up again.

One of the additional worries is that most mentally handicapped children have little or no sense of danger. They cannot anticipate it. Often they cannot say clearly who they are. If the child looks normal this makes matters even worse. If the child needs constant supervision but still escapes, the mother may be told, as Mrs Williams was, that she is not looking after the child properly.

Mrs Williams Before, he used to run out into the road anywhere.

CLH Has he got no sense of danger?

Mrs Williams No. He'd . . . climb anywhere. One day he was missing and was gone for two hours, we had the police out looking for him. They found him over at Blackmoor – sat in the middle of the road, he wouldn't move. But the policeman said someone must have seen him cross the busy roads. The times I've looked out there and seen buses stop and Bobby's just been standing in the road. And I pleaded with them, it was to do with this health visitor that came here, to get somebody to fence off the garden for me. Now they told me, if I bought the wood, they'd get the council to do it. I couldn't afford it! I mean, it would have cost the earth to have it up all around the back – 'cos that's all open and this is where he used to get out. Well then he got into the habit of just diving over the hedge and then he'd be out there where the buses stop. Talk about a cat with nine lives, I think he's had a hundred lives. The times he's been out on that road – and then somebody tells me I ought to look after him.

The description Mrs Shepherd gives of bringing up her mentally handicapped child seems fairly typical. It certainly corresponds quite closely with my own experience. Messy incidents before toilet-training is achieved really are upsetting, and one does not have to be 'anal fixated' to mind very much if there is excrement all over the place. Mrs Shepherd resorts to smacking and feels guilty afterwards. Then there is the conflict between allowing the child to do as much as possible for himself, or doing things for him because one is in a hurry. Here the school can achieve much; the pattern of 'Mummy do it' has not been established and the cool expectation that the child can do things for himself seems to produce results. This is why it is important to get the child to school early so that the right patterns can be impressed on his mind. Once the wrong ones are there, it is extremely difficult to alter them.

Mrs Shepherd He is eight and we have to dress him . . . and he still wears nappies at night . . .

Mr Shepherd We get on quite well, you couldn't possibly not get on with him, but it is more of an effort on your part to make him do things, to make him get up and walk around and go and play or sing. You have got to do things with him, otherwise he tends not to do much on his own.

Mrs Shepherd The thing is Stephen would come in and perhaps sit down for a couple of hours and do practically nothing, and then he would go on what we call a rampage round the house. He has definite things in each room that he does, especially in the kitchen – it is a sort of organized trip, but we are slowly managing to get a few things back on the shelf.

He still wears nappies at night but he is pretty good during the day. He has no speech at all . . . not a single word, not persistently, you know. The other morning I was getting him dressed and he came in and said 'clothes', as clearly as anything, but he has never said it since, and you can't get him to say it again.

Mrs Shepherd   You know, when we get these awful accidents, when he has lost his pants here, and I am not around and he takes them off, it means scrubbing everything practically from top to bottom and you just don't know where to start . . .

Mr Shepherd   We have tried, I think this is where the strain comes in really, you need one eye on him all the time, you know.

Mrs Shepherd   How do we control him? We try but it does not seem to work although they have said at school recently that he does get a bit more upset and he cries if they are really displeased, so this may be a sign of emotional development, but in the end if I take recourse to smacks I find that I feel very guilty afterwards. Actually I feel sometimes that one gets so tense that one does smack too hard.

To parents who have been deeply influenced by Spock and Winnicott, Mr Peters's account (below) of disciplining his child must make painful reading. Among middle-class parents, particularly, there is much emphasis on reasoning with the child. Instead of physical threats, speech is used as a weapon to bring normal children to order. The chaotic behaviour of the mentally handicapped infant brings out some of the fears many of us have about controlling children. Many times one feels that all discipline will break down if one does not 'draw a line somewhere'. With mentally handicapped children the lines of demarcation are less distinct and often the child will frighten one by his behaviour. With our own child we are frequently much more authoritarian than we would like to be and this is of course noticed by the other children. Our lack of consistency worries them at times and this must add to their sense of insecurity.

Mr and Mrs Peters's daughter, Mary, is four. Mr Peters felt that he must be the firm one of the two parents; that he must be the one to train the child to behave and to be disciplined. After a time he found this difficult because he could see the same fear in Mary's eyes as when he was training dogs (he is very fond of dogs and understands them). He felt he was treating the child too harshly and yet he could not help himself because he knew that his wife was desperate. His physical pain was always with him (from an industrial accident) and the banging, rocking and screaming of the child became too much for him. Their sleep was constantly interrupted because Mary would come into their bed at all hours. In the end he slept nearest to the door so that when Mary tried to get in he could take her back into her bed. He has been very strict and it hurts him when the child insists on going to her mother rather than to him.

In the house Mary is very difficult; she spills things, such as a whole tin of Vim, all over the place; the wall in the lounge had to be painted again because of the scribblings on the wall. Sometimes Mary runs into the street and then people who don't know about the brain-damage blame the parents as if they had been negligent.

The problem of looking after the child and preventing him from running away is illustrated by Mrs Hopkins. When the child does run off for a long time the police may have to be called. The parents will feel guilty at having caused so much fuss and bother; and there is the fear of accidents to himself or to others, or that he might lock himself in a car boot, for instance. There is very little appreciation of danger or anticipation of difficulty in a mentally handicapped child, and although one may know this rationally it is still not easy to anticipate each crisis, particularly if one wants the child to gain some independence. There remains the fear of spoiling the child, or of not sensing when he really needs help or when he is 'having everyone on'.

Mrs Hopkins's boy is capable of learning things. This is important and perhaps may show parents with younger children who are feeling depressed that there is progress, but this is hard to notice. Occasionally we say to each other, 'He couldn't (or wouldn't) have done that last year.'

Mrs Hopkins When he was a baby he took hours to feed and he couldn't burp without bringing up food, getting him on to solids was murder, but we did eventually. Now we can't stop him eating ... we had masses of advice on toilet-training but of course we didn't even attempt to toilet-train him for a long time and he wasn't clean and dry until his younger brother was clean and dry which must have been not until he was five. He was dry during the day-time except for occasional accidents, but he was still in nappies at night until he was almost five and he has continued to have accidents during the day and at night, but not quite so much at night as during the day until he was about seven. Now at the age of eight he takes himself to the toilet and he has very few unintended accidents.

If the parents of mentally handicapped children want them to make good progress, they must be prepared to devote themselves wholeheartedly to the task. When a living has to be earned and there are other children to be cared for, this is a tremendous task.

Mrs Hopkins Unless you happen to catch John at the moment when he is willing to learn he'll just get up and walk off or try to do something else. In order to try and teach him anything at all and to get him to co-operate you have to catch him in the right mood, often then you can teach him quite a lot. He's learnt a lot of little songs and his words are coming along quite nicely, and he can help tidy up and make a bed if he feels like it; if not, of course, he can turn the whole place upside down, pee all over the floor and things.

When John was very young we used to spend a lot of time exercising him and letting him pull himself up with

103

his hands and he made very fast progress until he was about a year old . . . his speech has been very, very slow. He had the odd sound at the usual time of about twelve to fifteen months, but it was not until he was quite old, about three, that he started to say one or two words. Now at the age of eight he has quite a good vocabulary and communicates quite well. This is one of the most difficult things to deal with because you can't leave him with strangers who are unable to communicate with him. It makes him very difficult if he can't communicate and he gets very, very cross and frustrated.

Holidays present a special problem. At home one can make some provision for dealing with an over-active child and be on guard against his tricks. On holiday everything is strange and exciting and for the parents it can be a nightmare rather than a holiday.

Mrs Hopkins The holiday was a great strain, particularly as John developed a tendency to run away at about the age of six. He was fairly easy to control when he was small as he couldn't get up the speed to run away but as he grew older and faster and I already had perhaps a baby in a pram and a toddler to look after, I found it more and more difficult to go out with the three children . . . Now he has discovered that he can open the front door by himself. We have fixed a chain but even so he gets a chair and gets at the chain . . . we are hoping that as he gets older he won't run away quite so much, I think he only wants to go out because he is bored.

This is one of the greatest of our problems: what to do with him at the weekends and during the holidays. He gets extremely bored . . . I find that except for one or two friends people will say 'Oh, yes, he went that way' but they wouldn't dream of stopping him. They just watch him go. He has been brought back, but on the whole people just tend to note that he has gone past and do nothing about it. He ran off to the zoo on one occasion and he must have looked very odd as he was wearing his little brother's shirt, stomach sticking out and a great gap in the middle. But apparently no one noticed him at the zoo or took him under control.

Mr and Mrs Jenkins seem to have less of a problem because Peter is a high-grade mongol, but it does show what a wide range of ability there is among mentally handicapped children. It is amusing to note that at the centre he is regarded as 'a feather in their cap'. The parents clearly are very keen to have him learn to read and write and their hopes may be realistic. With other parents it may be necessary to help them understand the limited aptitudes of their child. Sometimes it may be more important to develop other skills or to develop a system of priorities.

Mrs Jenkins   We treat Peter as a normal child. We know that he does things slower, but we still expect him to do things and he does them. We can take him out anywhere, but there again we were lucky, we have a high-grade mongol and usually he is pretty good, but if he decides he doesn't want to do something he won't . . .

Mr Jenkins   Small things sometimes, he might not want to eat his dinner. You say 'Come on now, eat those potatoes' and he'll say he doesn't like potatoes and you know he damn well loves potatoes, he can never eat enough of them, but he's just got that funny thing into his head that he won't eat them and he won't. We can let him out and leave him out there. We have told him enough times 'You can't go past the end of that road' and he will stay out there quite happy.

Mrs Jenkins   He writes his name, and he can write Mummy and Daddy, and Rose. There's even talk now of getting him to an ESN school . . . but the education authorities are holding it up, and at the centre they want him to go because it would be a feather in their cap, wouldn't it?

Mr Jenkins They say he might go for twelve months, but this has been going on since Christmas; the educational people are dragging their feet over it, but we shall be very pleased if he does because I think he could learn to read and write if he was pushed.

While the mentally handicapped child is at the chaotic stage, neither toilet-trained nor able to communicate verbally, either over-active or too passive, the rest of the family will be going through their worst time. It must depend a great deal upon where the family lives and how well-off it is. A child banging monotonously for more than half an hour at a time must cause resentment among neighbours if the family live in a flat; in any case the parents will feel self-conscious and guilty.

There is a great need for vastly increased nursery education for all children in this country. For mentally handicapped children the need is even more urgent and the fact that the pre-school period may be the worst for the parents should be noted by local authorities and social service agencies. Although, on the whole, good provision is made in many areas for the child over five, in many cases very little is done for the infants.

COMMENTS AND RECOMMENDATIONS

1. Opportunities for mothers to talk to each other in the presence of either doctors or social workers were found to be particularly helpful. Since all the mothers present have children with mental handicaps, no one can seem to have an advantage or could possibly be seen to be claiming some sort of superiority. It helps to know that there are others who are worse off, and one may pick up some useful advice. Doctors and social workers need to learn by direct experience how the problems are seen by members of the group. Group meetings save time and may prepare the ground for individual contact.

2. Nursery playgroups and nursery schools are urgently needed. Early stimulation is vital, time-consuming and often impossible for parents with other children. Nursery groups where mothers help will also provide a meeting-place for those with similar problems and a chance for mixing normal and handicapped children.

3. There are some good records which help with speech and movement; they may also stimulate interest as well as give some pleasure.

    Remember that the development of the mentally handicapped child is slower than that of the normal child, so that the age quoted in books for various activities may not be the appropriate one (see p. 167).

4. Other children should be encouraged to play with the handicapped child. They should be told what is the matter with the child and what he can and cannot do.

5. The over-active child may need tranquillizers at night, which in turn will give the rest of the family a good night's

sleep and make the child more manageable during the day. Activities such as swimming or visits to an adventure playground will stimulate the inert child and provide activity for the over-active child.

7 THE NEXT CHILD

Many mothers find it hard to believe that they can produce a perfect child and there are often fears before birth that something may be wrong with the baby. It is quite shattering when these fears are actually confirmed, and even more so when the first child happens to be mentally handicapped and the parents are young and want more children. Laplace, a French mathematician, seemed undisturbed by the bombardments during the siege of Paris in 1871; when asked why he was so calm, he replied that he walked under the cover of the law of probability. This kind of calm will disappear when disaster, however unlikely it may have seemed before, has actually struck.

Mr and Mrs Shepherd received genetic counselling, but since the results of the test only came up two months after the second child was born most of the benefits were lost. Mrs Shepherd's distrust of doctors is significant, as also is the great strain; something of which she was not aware at the time.

CLH How did you hear about the genetic counselling scheme?

Mrs Shepherd Do you know, honestly I can't think, we must have heard of it somewhere. We asked the doctor and he wrote off . . . people, medical people, said, 'You ought to have another baby, it couldn't happen another time.' Occasionally it does and I do feel they made a mistake over this because someone we know had a second handicapped baby and I have wondered many times what happens if someone has two mongols ... When we came to have the tests they were extremely helpful, they did a very extensive test ... blood tests, matching up the colour of your eyes and all sorts of things. They were extremely pleasant ... The only drawback was that six months passed before they actually fitted us in and by that time I was five months pregnant; and also the tests take five weeks and we were waiting for the results. They came two months after he [the second child] was born. So actually it was a period of stress for me, the latter part of my pregnancy, because they said the results would be in six weeks and they ended up by taking five months, and of course I was beginning to wonder if everyone was happy with the results ... I have a great distrust of doctors now; I am afraid because they hoodwinked us so much over Stephen. I found once or twice when he was small and had tonsillitis, I automatically wondered whether there was anything wrong with his heart. The doctor came and examined him and I would watch him like a hawk because the only way to get the truth is to watch his face and even then doctors manage to look impassive, don't they? But I have this distrust of doctors and really I don't believe a word they say.

CLH   Waiting for the second child was a strain?

Mrs Shepherd   I didn't appear the least bit worried. I didn't realize that I felt worried, but I must have I think, because I had high blood pressure which wasn't toxaemia, it was a nervous thing, and I ended up by having to stay in hospital.

Mr Shepherd   I don't think it showed too much but I was a bit worried, you know, because we still weren't sure and my wife was in and out of hospital like a yo-yo ... a couple of weeks in, a couple of weeks out and then she had to go in three weeks before the birth, quite some time ... my big problem was, you know, what am I going to do with Stephen. Again the authorities could come up with no help at all.

The Next Child

The physical handicap which occurred with Mrs Hopkins's second child was very hard to bear. In a way she seemed to suffer more that time because the event reactivated all the feelings that had come with the birth of the first, mentally handicapped, boy. Considered dispassionately, the defect was not only slight but soon cured; the difficulties at the time, however, were felt to be great and were probably not recognized because to all intents and purposes the baby was normal and very healthy.

Mrs Hopkins After we had genetic tests we had to make up our minds about having another baby and everybody said since the mongolism was of the erratic type there should be no danger whatsoever of the next child being a mongol. So we did decide to go ahead and have another baby. In a way, when the second child was born with a physical handicap, he had a bilateral dislocation of both hips, this was an even worse blow than John's mental handicap. (He was perfectly all right after eleven weeks in a metal frame, by the way.) I found that we were both very tense while I was pregnant with the second baby, and this, perhaps combined with the fact that he had a defect, made me resent the second baby and this may have made him difficult to deal with. He was a screaming baby who stayed awake at night and wanted constant feeding, cuddling and handling and this meant that John had a rather raw deal as obviously one's duty is towards the new baby.

Mrs Jenkins talks about her fear 'because I had one normal one, and one handicapped one, and I thought, well, it's more likely that I'll have another abnormal one now, you know'. When the last child was born it seemed ages to her before she was told that it was normal. To overworked doctors and nurses a couple of days may not seem a long time; for Mrs Jenkins it was an eternity before she knew that her new child was all right. When there has been a handicapped child in the family it might be a good idea to reassure the parents very quickly indeed, if this is possible. The waiting period will have been much harder for them to bear, and they may be considerably more tense than other parents.

CLH   ... and two years after you'd had the mentally handicapped one you decided to have the next child. Did you take any advice on this?

Mrs Jenkins   Well, the doctor just said, 'If I were you, I would have another baby right away.'

CLH   Was it a rough time waiting?

Mr Jenkins   Yes, it was.

Mrs Jenkins   Very much so.

Mr Jenkins   I can say it now. I think mentally she had a worse time with Beatrice, who is two years younger than Peter, than she did with the oldest.

Mrs Jenkins   We never bothered with counselling. No one suggested anything, so we didn't do anything.

CLH   Did you go and see a gynaecologist?

Mrs Jenkins   We saw a doctor, but he didn't suggest any tests or anything.

Mr Jenkins   No, he just told us to go ahead with it; all they did was to take blood tests of Peter ...

CLH   You said you were suffering, were you anxious?

Mrs Jenkins   Yes, I used to get awfully upset, crying, wondering what was going to happen. I was almost afraid when I had her, to ask. In fact, I didn't ask, I waited for them to say that she was perfectly all right.

CLH   Were they quick to tell you?

Mrs Jenkins   Well, they didn't tell me right away, not even then. The consultant came round one day and said I had a mongol child and said that this one was perfectly all right, and that was the first I had heard. I had been afraid to ask.

CLH   How long after the birth was that?

Mrs Jenkins   Only a few days because I was only in there for four days – it was probably a couple of days, that was all.

If I had asked they probably would have told me. They should have told me earlier.

It would seem that Mr and Mrs Peters badly needed the help of a geneticist, as well as information: what were the sorts of defects of the two mentally handicapped children of someone Mr Peters had heard of? Were these in any way like those of his child? Could one separate out the rational fears from the irrational? Mr Peters was certain that they would not have any more children: 'Once I make my mind up that's it.' Mrs Peters was less certain and seemed sad about the decision, but what really frightened them was the prospect of the nine months' wait and the fear that it could happen again. When deciding whether to have another child, genetic advice should be made available (perhaps more speedily than in the case of Mr and Mrs Shepherd) but it is not enough by itself; there must be explanation and counselling. What seems straightforward to an expert on genetics may not be so obvious to a non-scientist. Added to this there is the nine-month waiting period, which will seem to be a very long time for the parents. When there is another genetic defect, as in Mrs Hopkins's case, the distress will be very great because all the old feelings will come up again. In families where there is stability, confidence and mutual support these are stresses that will be overcome.

Although it was never discussed in the interviews one may assume that in some instances the birth of a mentally handicapped child will make for sexual difficulties between husband and wife. Neither the fear of pregnancy nor all the depression and distress can be conducive to a happy sex life.

The worst thing is the period of waiting for the next child: all the couples who went ahead and had another child mentioned this. We found it very reassuring to be told immediately that our last child was not a mongol or abnormal in any way; even two days' waiting seemed too long to Mrs Jenkins.

1. Birth control must be used from the moment the couple resume sexual relations. Therefore advice on contraceptives and family planning is essential as soon as possible after birth. With many doctors and clinics this is standard practice, but it cannot be taken for granted. After the birth of the mentally handicapped child there may well be fears of conception and therefore an increase in general tension. Good advice on contraception may lessen this tension.

   If information on birth control is not readily available locally ring the Family Planning Association (see p. 172) and they will tell you where you can find help in your part of the country. The Brook Advisory Clinic will do the same. Ring their London head office (see p. 171).

2. The most common fear is that the next child will also be abnormal. The best way of allaying this fear is to have genetic counselling, and for this to be useful it must be given *before* the next pregnancy. Not all parents will know about this sort of advice, which we certainly found to be invaluable. Hospitals, doctors, midwives and health visitors should be provided with information about the availability of genetic counselling.

   Your doctor should be able to tell you where the nearest centre for genetic counselling is, and give you a letter to take to the centre. Should you be unable to obtain this information from your doctor, write to MIND Exchange (see p. 173).

3. Parents should be told immediately after the birth of the next child whether or not there is any degree of handicap, or whether this is suspected.

8 THE CHILD GROWS UP

As the child grows up there are bound to be new problems and what has been acceptable before becomes less easy to tolerate. As the child moves into adolescence, he will grow larger, stronger and more difficult to control physically. When David was small, in the last resort I could just pick him up and carry him from one place to another. When he was thirteen he had become large and certainly overweight and if he made up his mind not to be moved, no one could move him.

Sexual development comes with adolescence and even with 'normal' young people this is not an easy time. Sexual development cannot be concealed or denied: voices break, breasts develop, beards sprout and there are new tensions. The unpleasant aspects of puberty which we have all gone through, and often try to forget as best we can, underline the worst things about having a mentally handicapped child: that pregnancy might be a possibility, but that marriage, grandchildren and the conventional expectations of parents are not for us.

The mentally handicapped are not exempt from the swings of mood, rebellious feelings and depressions which characterize adolescence and which are part of growing up. Parents have to face up to physical growth, moods and rebelliousness at a time when they are less energetic and flexible. It is much easier to accept the sexuality of young people than it used to be; nevertheless, when it comes to one's own children it is not all that easy to discuss or seek help when sexual tensions and difficulties crop up. It seems that adolescence is another watershed, a time when old tensions are reawakened and the possibility arises that a previously manageable child is now approaching adulthood unable to deal with all the demands of growing up.

Jane has always been extremely difficult to deal with; she is not typical but her case highlights what some families have to face up to. Mrs Taylor described some of the problems:

Mrs Taylor   I used to have little messages sent home via the minibus about Jane's behaviour: today she scratched a child all down the face; today she pulled someone's hair. I became very unhappy because soon it became very, very clear that some other arrangements would have to be made for her. We waited for two years for a place at the hospital. At the time we didn't have a clue why there were behaviour problems. On one occasion I was talking to another parent and she was able to inform me that Jane wasn't in her old class. Years later we heard from a member of staff how disastrous that move was. She seemed to feel it had been left too late. Had they moved Jane to another class earlier it might have worked. Then we were referred to my social worker who is exceptionally good. I was grateful to have him because I have had a stream of others and they were a dead loss. He got us an appointment at the hospital. The doctor there flatly refused to have Jane's name entered on the waiting-list for hospital day-care. You see, the headmistress of Jane's school had said, on taking up her post, that there was no child, *no child* that one could not educate. And now the doctor was complaining that she had received a list of children from her for the hospital waiting-list! As we were leaving, the doctor had a change of mind and said that Jane was to be accepted on the waiting-list – but we weren't to think that Jane could become a resident at the hospital later in life. Then we moved house, out of the catchment area. We thought, surely after waiting for two years this would be taken into consideration . . . the new hospital said no way, it's not now our policy to have children taken into hospital anyway – we had to laugh, otherwise we would have screamed. First of all it was decided that Jane needed hospital care and then my social worker had a letter from our hospital to say, 'We are sorry. Now that you have moved out of our catchment area her name must come off the list.' It all had to start all over again. So I said to my social worker, 'Find out which hospital area we are living in.' It took some time and she was most apologetic. She said, 'Apparently the top half of our area comes into one area and the bottom half into another; your road runs from top to bottom and you live in the middle of the road and you don't come into any of them' – this is true, this is as it stands at the moment.

Recently, I telephoned the social services and told them to come and fetch Jane. I was in a most distressed condition. At the time I phoned, Jane was attacking my mother and she had mum by the hair and she had pulled her right across the room. The social worker who was on emergency duty came. I telephoned the vicar, too. He has been very, very kind and I told him what I had done. I regretted telephoning, thinking, what sort of mother am I? I said, 'Look, I am having all sorts of problems with my feelings, I feel as if I wish she would die and then later I wish I hadn't felt like this.' The social worker said, 'Mrs Taylor, you're not in a fit state to make a decision', and the vicar said to her, 'Fit state to make what decision? Mrs Taylor made a decision years ago and that was that she could not cope with this child any longer, day in and day out . . .' They managed to get her into hospital for the weekend from Friday night to the Sunday afternoon.

Eventually Jane was admitted to a boarding school. The local authority helped with the fees because their school had refused to take Jane. The holidays remained a nightmare.

There was a playgroup which took Jane from the home for four or five hours. Here Mrs Taylor describes what happens when Jane is at home:

Mrs Taylor   It depends on the mood really. One can't win because if she is in a good mood it's mischief and all sorts of things happen. Things are thrown out of the window over into the garden next door. The sugar is tipped out, the water is turned on in the bathroom. That's in a good mood.

Mr Taylor   It's her strength. She can drag someone like you right across the room; it hurts my wife to see how I handle her; there is no doubt about it, I have to match strength for strength. She will either injure herself or someone else, possibly another child.

Mrs Taylor   The specialist at the hospital said, 'Do you think Jane is naughty because she is trying to draw attention to herself and it would be better if you completely ignored her?' and I said to him, 'Yes, I quite agree but what am I to do when I am out in the street and she attacks a child? Am I to say to the mother, "I am expected to completely ignore this sort of behaviour?" You can't, you can't be consistent.'

As Jane started her periods and became a young woman, another dimension to the problems of living with her emerged.

Mrs Taylor   She started her periods when we had her at home. My one fear was her habit of stripping herself and I worried dreadfully over this. We have lads living upstairs and she went into our bedroom and removed her sanitary towel and she left it draped all over . . .

Mr Taylor   When we are out, we have to march into the Gents. She refuses to go with her mother and I have to take her . . . Being self-employed I have lost a lot of work and therefore a lot of money. So I have said I am going back into employment. My employers will be forced to sack me because of the hours I miss and I shall go on the State.

In cases like this one, and it can't be the only one, it is no use advocating the abolition of hospitals for the subnormal. The burden of looking after a girl like Jane must be shared by professionals. One cannot rely on student volunteers. They can relieve the family for a few hours and they are often marvellous with the handicapped, but like all students they move on to lead their own lives and follow their own careers and they may be succeeded by another generation of students less concerned with the handicapped; fashions in social concern change.

In many ways the Armitage family might be considered fortunate. Their son, Rory, has been to a Steiner school since the age of four and will most probably be looked after for the rest of his life. It depends on the local authority who are paying the fees. The pain and the problems to the parents seem to continue, however. I interviewed them during the holidays.

Mrs Armitage   They break up at the end of June and he goes back in the middle of August. Then they have a holiday for the first fortnight in October. At the moment he is in a wonderful hostel; the wardens, a married couple, they are excellent. There are a lot of things Rory can do. He can wash himself. He can dress himself. But will he? You've got to be standing over him – it's the same with everything. You see, any job you give him to do, if you walk away his concentration just goes. He can be just too embarrassing. A case in point: we went to do some shopping and he didn't want to go; usually he likes pushing the trolley, but he didn't want to go. At the counter there was a queue, he didn't want to wait and so he started shouting, he flung himself on the floor in front of people. I mean, he is nearly sixteen. When he was a little boy people were rude to us; they'd turn round and say, 'That kid wants a good hiding.' Now he is fully grown you just can't get away with it and the trouble is that he looks so normal. The other day I was at a swimming pool and there was a mongol girl who was going round picking up everyone's shoes, taking them back to her mother. The mother would bring them back and no one would say a word, and I said then, 'If that had been Rory they would all have complained and said something' ... Now he does all these embarrassing things when we are out; it doesn't worry my husband half as much as it worries me; when it happens with me I just want to curl up into a ball and die; I feel now I can't take any more of it. It has come to the point that I don't want to take him out any more because I am so frightened ...

Mrs Taylor also spoke of this lack of confidence which had overtaken her over the years: '... the thing I have noticed most is that I have no confidence, I never had much and what I had has been drained away by Jane'.

Relationships with husbands were also raised.

Mrs Taylor   I might as well speak frankly; our marriage is non-existent because for the last few years we have had to lead separate lives, and gradually you drift apart. It's inevitable, something has to go.

Mr Taylor   Your whole family is split, you see. You take it out on the boy [Jane's adopted brother]; you have a fight between yourselves and you tend to take it out on him when Jane is in a mood. We love her dearly.

Mrs Taylor   But the problems of friction between each other – you see we took this house when we thought Jane was going to be catered for, knowing that we had to renovate it. It is in a dreadful condition and I say, 'When are you going to make a start on the house?' and he says, 'When *you* look after her,' and of course I say, 'I can't', and I burst into tears.

The Armitages explained how during the 'holiday' one crisis seemed to follow another.

Mr Armitage I went down and there he was by the deckchair, scraping about in the dirt. Well, he came in and I said, 'You'd better come and see this! I've taken his trousers off and they were soiled.'

Mrs Armitage The thing was, he was so obsessed with what he was doing, he couldn't be bothered to break off and go . . .

Mr Armitage And so he soiled himself; then he panicked, so he'd taken his trousers down and sat down, then he decided to put his trousers back on. There it was, all the dirt and the gravel and the grass in his pants . . . this is a lad who is physically as strong as me.

Mrs Armitage At school they say he doesn't do that sort of thing much.

Mr Armitage Well, they say this is a child crying out for attention. I can't give him any more.

The relationships with brothers and sisters were discussed. Obviously there are bound to be problems in all families between the various members, particularly during adolescence, but a mentally handicapped child adds further stress.

Mr Armitage My daughter, yes, she's very bright, she has never had a failure in her life.

Mrs Armitage I would go so far as to say she is rather hard.

Mr Armitage The hardness is there, although she has never kicked out against Rory being handicapped or complained about it, but if I was in her place I would. It's bad enough having a mongol [until this interview I had never considered that I had been particularly fortunate!] but Rory looks normal enough and comes in and uses terribly vulgar expressions to Rachel's young friends because he sees them laughing and wants to join in and be one of them, though he's no idea what he's really said.

How can she continue to have friends in? I think it has had the effect of stopping her bringing people home here ... but we have never entertained much in this house ...

Mrs Armitage We've had parties.

Mr Armitage Well, we had parties on birthdays, but for God's sake, two in ten years, it's a bit ... you know.

As the Taylors' lives were affected more profoundly by the disturbance Jane was creating, their son was also suffering more intensely. The fact that he had been adopted added to his parents' feelings of guilt.

Mrs Taylor Before we adopted him we thought of everything, whether he would be affected, would Jane do any damage ... But one thing we never thought of was that Alan might start a series of headaches when we moved to this house. I was absolutely convinced that it wasn't anything physical. The doctor didn't think it was anything physical either. Alan came home from school one day, and – it's quite a regular occurrence – I was in tears; he just looked at me and he walked out, and when he came back he was cutting a grapefruit and he said, 'Here you are, mummy, I've bought this for you. Don't worry, I'll look after you', and it was then that I became aware that he was so concerned for me, coming home day after day, seeing me in floods of tears, that the little chap was taking this burden ...

Mr Taylor These holidays we have noticed that there aren't any of his friends around here, not because they won't come but because he tells them not to. When Jane is away he will come in the car and we'll take the dog on to the sands and run around. When Jane is at home he just pulls a face and won't go anywhere. He won't say anything. He is embarrassed – more deeply than we know, more than he talks about.

Mr and Mrs Danby are over seventy years old and their son,

Roy, seemed to cause few difficulties. The main problem seemed to be the prospect of death and sickness and the knowledge that neither of them could cope much longer. They had few complaints and emphasized their independence and their standards.

Mr Danby Marriage is not as sacred as it was in our day. A marriage today, well, they're married one day and divorced the next, or living apart. Yes, we see our life through the Sunday School. You attended Sunday School, and you married for keeps. We stick together, we get our ups and downs. We get our problems and we've got to face them ... I wouldn't term myself a good Christian. As I say, we have to face facts and these problems come when we get older. I do get bitter but it doesn't make it any better. Each day a problem crops up. Yesterday's goes and another one comes the next day. We have always got the worry of Roy. I am thinking now that if anything happened to either of us, what is going to happen to him? ... I've never applied for anything because I was fortunate really. I didn't have big money but I was never out of work. I never lost a day's pay in my life – not that that's anything to boast about. At any rate we have always done our best. One or two people think we have been marvellous with Roy. Well, it's nice to think that people feel that but they don't realize what it involves socially ... at our age, I mean, we should be getting about together. We've always got to think of him. One or the other has to be at home for him. Not that we mind, we don't, we have accepted it all our lives, haven't we?

Mrs Danby I haven't wanted to do anything else but look after him. We used to have different people come to visit us. Not very often, just to see if everything was all right, but of course we never bothered with them, we always did everything for ourselves ... We only get the attendance allowance, but we've got nothing to grumble about.

123

Mr Danby It seemed to me that my hardest struggle was before the attendance allowance came in. My wage wasn't a big wage but of course the family came first; as I say, we are the older sort of people. We don't look for the gay life. I mean home is home to us and that's where our pleasure lies. I go in for a TV and that's our pleasure, where some people go out and spend pounds on a night's drinking, Bingo and all that . . . What I do find is that we lack a lot of things socially. There was an invitation from the firm I was working for, well, we can't leave him. I've said 'I'm sorry we can't come, we've got Roy . . .'

Going back many years, they took us to see that hospital and we had a look around and I said, 'As long as I have a breath in my body he won't go.' You see, places like that, they're institutions and not the same as the hostels they have got now. If you could see that hostel where Roy goes sometimes, it's marvellous. It's home from home. Roy is happier there than here, you see he has the company of his own kind. If they said, for argument's sake, next week that there was a permanent place for him, we should have to get over the hurt of being without him. If anything happens to us, well it has to come some time or other, I'd feel happy and contented with the fact that I knew he was in a place like that . . .

My wife's sister, she has just lost her husband, they only had one son but he is married now, happily married and they have got two nice children. It's something we shall never experience, grandchildren.

It was sad that the Danbys had not been able to see their way to sending their son to the hostel sooner. The shadow of the workhouse, memories of public scandals about 'mental hospitals' and their own sturdy independence made it impossible for them to liberate themselves from the burden of having a mentally handicapped son. Admittedly he was not a great deal of trouble and did not really need a hospital; the hostel was just the right sort of place for him. It seems a shame that the parents, even at their age, could not be offered a place for Roy.

Mr and Mrs Davis had just sent their son to the subnormality hospital. Mr Davis had retired.

Mr Davis What with sleepless nights and other problems, I never had a weekend to myself. I'm sixty-two, the opportunity arose and now I have enjoyed a year and a half of retirement and I have no regrets.

Mrs Davis I could not cope any more, it just became increasingly tiring. The days grew longer and longer. He didn't go to bed until ten and he didn't go to sleep until midnight or later. The doctor kept changing his drugs. He started taking his clothes off during the evening and coming down here just to draw our attention and then his toilet habits got a bit out of hand as well. As we were getting older he was getting older too; he was getting bored with us. When we went out he got naughtier, snatching ladies' baskets and things like that. He would go up to any small child and grab their wrists, wanting them to pat his head. There was this big boy towering over them, frightening them out of their wits . . . It got to such a pitch that I took him to see the doctor one week and he said, 'Look, it's really time he went away, is he on anyone's list?' So Christopher went to the hospital and he has settled down remarkably well.

Mr Davis We left him there to settle down and when eventually after about six weeks we took him out, he waved us goodbye without a moan. There is a day-room with fitted carpets and a television set. They have a room, just two of them, because he has made a friend who is older, who can talk perfectly well. He is not a mongol or anything like that, I don't know what's the matter with him. He is called Jim, he's very fond of music and he helps Christopher with his cassettes, and they said, 'These two are getting on so well that we'll put them together.' He has never had a friend in his life, you see. It really is better, better than the Home Farm Trust, there is a new wing. He has taken all his own clothes, all his records and tapes. Everything he possessed has gone. They've already bought him new clothes ... I defend this place; people who have never been near criticize. At meetings or anything like that I just step in and ask, 'Have you been? Have you seen the place? Because it's not as bad as you say, you should not criticize unless you have been to see for yourself.'

As we were discussing adolescence and adult life, sexual matters inevitably cropped up but were not discussed in great detail. This is hardly surprising as most of the parents hardly knew me and I did not want to push the interview beyond the limits of their tolerance. Sexual development is yet another reminder that everything is wrong: lasting relationships may not easily be formed, the mentally handicapped may well notice that they can shock or draw attention to themselves and the parents dread pregnancy or the possibility that their child may be sexually assaulted. When there are friendships the parents are not sure how to handle them.

I asked Mr Strachey about Clive's development.

CLH He is a young man now; has this made life more difficult?

Mr Strachey Only as he goes off into his bedroom and is up there for an hour at a time. He is acting as an adult up there. And also the fact that he keeps changing his clothes ...

Mrs Strachey He takes off his clothes, shirts and ties and things. I have to wash things ...

Mr Strachey He certainly recognizes girls. I tease him, 'What about that girl then, Clive?' He colours up. He looks at them like a normal boy. Sometimes the girls say 'Hello' to him and I say, 'Who's that?' and he'll say, 'I don't know'.

126

CLH   How would you feel about it if he had a girl-friend?

Mrs Strachey   There is a young woman, she's twenty-eight, goes to the Centre, pushes herself on to Clive.

Mr Strachey   She holds his hand.

Mrs Strachey   But it's all her, not Clive, no, because one night they were sitting in the car and Clive was right in the corner and she was leaning over him, she's a big girl. It worries him. 'Come on,' she says and he sits there, he cowers in the corner of the car. But when they come out of the Centre they walk along hand-in-hand, but she obviously has got hold of his hand and made him do it.

It seemed to me that the parents looked on this relationship in the sort of way that most parents would, teasing, and certain that the girl was the forward one. When I pressed, Mr Strachey agreed that he had been talking about masturbation when he mentioned that Clive went up to his room for hours at a time.

Mrs Howard's daughter, Denise, also went to a training centre. Her mother was worried about her being too friendly, too indiscriminate.

Mrs Howard   She speaks to everyone and they will stop and chat. This worries me a lot because she went through a spell of wanting to hug everyone. I accepted this because if I ever go to the Centre they come from all directions wanting to hug me. I felt that this is just something we have to live with, it's just part of being handicapped. Denise went up to one of the staff and she was pushed away, and I thought this was just awful. I talked to this woman afterwards and I said Denise was unhappy and we were getting complaints about her bad temper. I said, 'No wonder she is in a bad temper if she gets pushed away.' The lady said they were trying to stop all this hugging because last week the lemonade delivery men came and she went up to one of these young lads and put her arms round him. So of course they thought it was time to stop the hugging because it could have the wrong effect. Of course I said 'I haven't been told all about this', and it seemed so cruel suddenly . . .

At the time Denise was going to the shops. I would give her a little note and she would pop off down to the shops, no problem at all. Then suddenly one day I went to the gate and there was a young man coming down the road; Denise ran and put her arms round him and he was terribly embarrassed. I rushed over and brought her back and it dawned on me, she couldn't go out alone any more. I tried to explain: 'You must not do it, it's all right inside the family but outside you must not hug, ladies don't do that . . .' It's taken a few years.

Right at the end of the interview Mrs Howard came back to the problem and it became clear that she had not just been over-protective; there was a real cause for her anxiety, but it took a long time and clearly some effort to bring herself to talk.

Mrs Howard I waited for her and I was searching around and eventually I found her sitting on a wall; she was crying. For some reason they had let her out early and she came out at four. There is a shop at the end of the lane and the man there had always been nice, chatted to her, given her an orange, a few sweets or something. It seemed that she was coming home alone and he had called her, given her an orange or something, and then took her out to the back and sexually assaulted her. So we got the police and told them the whole thing and in the end they said, 'Well, she can't speak clearly enough or explain, and we can't really bring charges.' She couldn't go to court and give evidence. And the things the man said; he said she had gone into the shop and stolen something. He was definite about that and she couldn't deny it. A police-woman came that night and they went into the kitchen alone and she was very good. I know it happened. They said, 'You can insist on taking it to court . . . but she can't stand up and say anything.' Strangely, the man was later found guilty of raping a young child that lived next door at the time.

That was the one time I didn't meet her because they sent them home early. Amazing isn't it? Lots of people think I am over-protective. But I also feel for other people. She's very fond of babies, always wanting to hug them or hold them. Most mothers were very good and they would chat to her at her level but sometimes she would go and pick up the little one, then it became frightened because she was a stranger and I would come to the rescue. I wished that a few would tell her off. I said 'If you touch a baby we come straight home', and we did that several times and then it stopped.

Denise was twenty-one years old. Her maternal instinct had to be thwarted, her natural friendly hugs had to be stopped and she had been sexually assaulted. Confusion can arise when affection is mistaken for sexual advances. With mentally handicapped men it may be mistaken for a sexual advance when there is no such intention. This sums up the problem of the sexuality of the mentally handicapped. The need is there, the urge – usually not as strong as with the majority of adults – exists and it is not easy just to ignore it. It is not a question of being old-fashioned or inhibited but it is important to consider the standards of the community and what it is possible for a family to tolerate. It would seem to me that if masturbation can be done in private it is quite reasonable to allow it, indeed it may well relieve tension and make a lonely person feel good. A warm and loving relationship between two mentally handicapped people should be acceptable and encouraged. The difficulty is to consider how contraceptive advice can be given and appropriate behaviour taught. The Family Planning Association has for years run a course on Sex Education and Personal Relationships for people working with mentally handicapped young people. The fear of sexuality is real and so is the need to express these feelings. It is certainly not a topic which is discussed comfortably. It would be useful if those living and working with the mentally handicapped could meet to discuss difficulties and attitudes. Sexual frustration must be related to other behaviour problems. None of the parents I interviewed talked about sexual difficulties spontaneously, but it became clear that Jane Taylor caused her parents much embarrassment when her periods began. Denise Howard was too affectionate and Clive Strachey went upstairs for long periods to masturbate and wanted to join in when other teenagers were 'messing about'.

COMMENTS AND RECOMMENDATIONS

1. The sexuality of young mentally handicapped people presents problems to all who work with them. If we believe in the rights and the dignity of the mentally handicapped, we should include the right to sexual pleasure and satisfaction, if that is at all possible. If sexual satisfaction is denied, young adults may become more bad-tempered and difficult to control. Those who deny sexual feelings should probably examine their own attitudes. The difficulty is not only that the mentally handicapped do not understand what we want them to understand, but also that our own attitudes get in the way. Young people can sense our unease. It might help parents to read Jane Cousins's *Make It Happy* (Penguin). It is written for young people, the language is frank, technical terms are explained and moral judgements avoided. The book could form the basis for discussion in groups of parents and professional helpers.

2. Sex education is possible but it must start early. It might be best to identify a number of things which need to be explained, such as the sex differences between men and women. Just as the mentally handicapped can learn to eat and dress in a socially acceptable manner, they may also be taught to learn the social customs related to sexual behaviour.

3. Physical changes such as menstruation may frighten girls and, because they do not understand what is happening, their behaviour may attract confusing reprimands. In the same way as toilet-training can be achieved, girls should if possible be taught to take care of themselves when they have periods. It may be possible to regulate periods with

131

the help of the pill. Mentally handicapped adults can of course conceive and their innocence and need for affection may lead to exploitation. Birth control must be considered seriously and here Brook Clinics, Family Planning Clinics or the G.P. may be consulted.

4. For boys, erections and ejaculation should be treated as acceptable matters. Gradually, using the careful behaviour modification approach advocated by Janet Carr (see p. 167), boys and girls can be encouraged to masturbate in private. If any sexual incident causes shock and upheaval it is quite likely that the undesirable behaviour will continue. Anything may be better than being ignored. Strong reproaches and punishment will not work. In any case masturbation is far too pleasant to stop just because of a telling-off!

For help, addresses and books, see pp. 167–72.

9 SCHOOL AND TRAINING CENTRE

The amount of help that parents receive from outside the home varies tremendously. It emerged fairly clearly from the interviews I had, that the more educated and articulate the parents were, the more likely they were to get help in the form of playgroups and so on. Where provisions are scarce or inadequate, it seems that those parents who stand up and claim their rights are the ones who get most help and support. The parents I talked to were relatively self-reliant and competent people and yet a frequent statement is summed up by 'whatever help we have had, we have had to fight for'. The harder help is to come by, the more difficult and 'fight-minded' the parents will become. In the end these parents will get less, and may become isolated, because the authorities in turn become suspicious and defensive.

The three working-class families I interviewed certainly had a worse time of it than the other parents. It would be rash on the basis of three interviews to generalize about the availability of provision, but there is a good deal of evidence elsewhere that even the standard benefits the Welfare State offers are not taken up sufficiently by working-class people. Sometimes the authorities seem to conserve scarce resources, instead of saying to their clients: 'This, this and this is what you are entitled to'. No one had ever come to the parents with a check-list (if indeed it had ever existed) and said to them 'Get what you can, you need it.' For example: a year after payment of the attendance allowance started, Mrs Williams had only just heard about it from her niece.

There is a great deal of evidence of help that was given readily and kindly, and some could be described as 'exceeding the call of ordinary duty'. But in the experience of our own family, although we can say that we have been helped a great deal, the initiative has always come from us. As I mentioned in the first chapter, when David was nearly driving us to despair because of his unceasing activity we asked for an interview with a consultant who prescribed a tranquillizer and added the splendid message: 'It does not matter whether he takes it or you, it's quite harmless.' In fact the provision of the tranquillizer was a turning point: we had better nights because the child slept, therefore we were better at handling him and he responded by being less anarchic. Why had not one of the agencies that helped us mentioned tranquillizers before?

The enormous benefits of the special school emerge clearly. They are essential for the handicapped child. Without the help of the teachers the children would make less progress (although Mrs Mercer is not as positive as the other parents on that point). Surely the school and the parents must aim at approaching the problem of education jointly rather than separately. There are difficulties in communication that are entirely understandable: the distance of the school from many homes, the fact that the children can't talk and that the staff are engaged in working with particularly demanding children. But more consultation and a joint approach to the whole problem would help parents and inevitably also the teachers. The parents interviewed here feel exhausted and often discouraged. Surely greater involvement would give them the feeling that they can play a part? Two parents mention a course of speech therapy that was really appreciated. Swimming in the school pool (if there is one) helps because the child can swim with water-wings and this sense of achievement is carried over into other activities. In all schools, parental involvement has been proved to be useful. This involvement now includes representation on the board of governors. I cannot see how long-term decisions can be made by people who have no direct acquaintance with the problems of having mentally handicapped children.

Being asked what one really needs is more desirable than an authority deciding what is good for the parents and then being surprised and hurt if the parents want something different.

Once Mrs Williams had got her son into a school for educationally subnormal children, improvement was tremendous.

Mrs Williams This particular health visitor that we had kept promising that Bobby was going to school after Christmas. That was in 1969. Everything was all arranged. Christmas came, but no letter to say Bobby was starting school. This is what I was palmed off with all the time, but then we had another health visitor and she's very nice but she doesn't come here any more, for what reason I don't know, but this was the one that tried to get Bobby on holiday last year. She has stopped coming to the house now . . . it's really the teachers at the school who are more interested in him now, and the psychologist over there.

CLH Are you pleased with the school?

Mrs Williams Oh yes, I reckon it's marvellous. Well, what they've done for Bobby over there, considering he was an absolute little terror when he started.

Mrs Jenkins (talking about Peter's admission to a school when he was three-and-a-half). Well the health visitor kept on at me to go and see the headmistress and I sort of put it off and put it off, I didn't want to go. I don't know why. Well in the end she said 'I'll come and take you down' and after that it was all right. I didn't know what to expect and I suppose the longer I kept him away, well, I could imagine to myself that he was normal, but I knew he wasn't. Once he did go he was ever so happy and he loved it, it was better for him.

Mr Jenkins It was a small place. We knew all the teachers personally. My wife said hello to the headmistress every morning and you felt part of the school. We met quite a lot of people, we had quite a lot of functions and everybody used to help; it was much easier to get involved because everybody felt, you got the impression, that they wanted you to.

CLH   What helped and what did not?

Mrs Mercer   Well, we had a health visitor but quite frankly she wasn't much help. The first thing she said was, 'My dear, if the baby had to be born somewhere it was a good thing he was born into this family' which wasn't a great help and that's about the only thing she said. Anyway we are very grateful for going to the doctor, we talked about anything you liked. I think looking back on it, it was simply the fact that you thought that somebody was interested in you and the baby. You know you forget to ask something, and you think 'I will ask that next time I go', and I have talked to other parents who haven't had this, and you know, the child could be three before they know there are any special facilities for caring for them at all. So I think we were rather lucky that way. She put us in touch with the National Society for Mentally Handicapped Children and I think I joined when Philip was only two months old and she told us all about the school, the workshop and everything. At that time I was convinced he would never sit up, he would never do anything. I thought I was going to feed a vegetable for the rest of my life. Dr Smith told us of many mongol children she had known, and she talked about it – I think she let us talk more than tell us things; you talk about your fears, and of course you see every time we went, she would open her book and say, 'Let me see, a month ago he was doing this and that, now he is doing something else.' It made you realize that he was making progress. Now Philip goes to school.

CLH   Do you feel you have been involved enough in the operation?

Mrs Mercer   No, I don't. I was very pleased when they did that speech course last year which we went to, and over a year we have at least got him to repeat words with us; at least he is learning to use words. I think you feel that you are useless, that you are helpless, not being able to help him. I would like to help him. I would like to see more junior schools, actually, so that we weren't all shoved down there [about eight miles away] because it is impossible to get to the school easily. Lack of transport stops me from going. I went once to join in the swimming. I think it started about 2 p.m. I know I had to leave here at 12.30 ... and I didn't get back until 4 o'clock. Well, I just can't do it.

Several points made by Mrs Mercer should be stressed. In the first place she had the support of a doctor who took an exceptional interest in parents with mongol children. She was able to talk to her about 'anything you liked' – it takes time to absorb information, especially when one is anxious.

When the number of possible consultations is limited there is always the fear that one has forgotten something and many questions are thought of after the interview is over. The interviewer may be very conscientious and say 'Have you any further questions?' but even that implies that time is running a bit short.

Middle-class people are much more competent in this sort of situation; they may even bring a check-list and work through it. What those in authority must realize is that if they really want to help the client he must be allowed to talk in his own way. Just a cheery 'no problems this week?' will produce a good turnover of clients but may not be much use to the individual.

Mrs Mercer did not have much help when she formed a playgroup. Local authorities will often conceal the names of parents with mentally handicapped children, which I am sure is wrong and out-of-date. It underlines that something is wrong which they feel guilty about, and prevents one of the things parents most appreciate: the opportunity to meet others with similar problems, to realize that they are not alone and that there is, in many cases, some progress and hope. This is the valuable function that the NSMHC performs, but if they are not given the names to make an approach some parents may be isolated for too long. Of course there must be an opportunity for anonymity, and here medical ethics may complicate the issue, but a distinction must be made between discretion and mystification for its own sake. Mrs Mercer could only point out the need by forming a playgroup, but this should be done officially and with all possible speed as a right rather than on the initiative of one rather exceptional mother.

Mrs Hopkins is also for the most part enthusiastic about school.

Mrs Hopkins We first heard about the school through the clinic and we were actually told by a neighbour that it might be that they would take our child who was then three and a half. Apparently the clinic at that time did not know that they took very young children and thought that they only went at five, but I understand that the clinics have been brought up-to-date on this. However, if a neighbour hadn't happened to mention this to us we would perhaps not have realized that John could go to the centre quite so early. So we got him to school when he was three years and nine months. It was one of the reasons why we couldn't undertake the conception of the third child . . . We couldn't find a playgroup for John. I think it was before Mrs Mercer was running hers for mentally handicapped children. I was at first pregnant and then had a new baby to look after and so I wasn't able to undertake much in that line either, so we were very grateful to the principal of the school when she said she would have John. But it would have been lovely if we could have formed some sort of playgroup earlier on for him to run around in.

Five is the normal age for admission to a school, though clearly exceptions have been made to this and the help was deeply appreciated. For whatever reason, some parents fared worse than others and the Richards and Peters families are less enthusiastic about the support they have received than the Hopkins and Mercer families. As the Shepherds show, the authorities can be forced to make statutory provisions but these can be pretty poor. I cannot imagine what good a twenty-two-mile bus ride did their child.

CLH Did you ask for admission to a school?

Mrs Shepherd Yes, I did actually, and they fobbed us off rather. They said he is making such good progress at home and you are obviously supplying all the right toys, which we were actually, so there is really no need for him to go.

Mr Shepherd We had a bit of difficulty in getting him in at five, yes, we had to push and press and that sort of thing. But I think that was because we were in —shire; well, their excuse was that they hadn't any room. We said well, he is five now, you have got to provide something. We had to send him on a journey of twenty-two miles every day, there and back again.

Mrs Shepherd It used to take about two hours, didn't it?

Mr Shepherd Two hours there and two hours back, but we felt that we had made our stand; that was all they had to offer and we had to accept it, didn't we?

Mrs Shepherd Nobody ever backed us in anything.

Mr Shepherd No, not there; we found things much better here. Compared with what we had before we find the school here very good and I like the teachers. I know they are very young, but I like the happy atmosphere there and I like the meetings they have there – the ones when you go down to discuss things. Actually I think it would be nice if we did that more often. But there again, if I found I wanted to pop down and collect him I felt quite free and welcome.

Mr Peters feels strongly that what help they have had, they have had to fight for. He has been able to get Mary into a special care unit for two days a week, but the parents think that this is too short to start any adequate training programme and in any case Mr Peters feels that this sort of help is only for a special 'clique' and not their sort. In a way he knows that this is not the case, but says that he begins to believe this when he has to argue about his rights all the time.

Mrs Peters had difficulty in getting Mary into a playgroup. The first help she got was when she heard that Mrs Mercer's playgroup had been formed, and saw a feature on television. She finds the playgroup a help because there are other mothers with similar problems.

Mrs Davis Whenever I asked for help the doctor gave it immediately. When Christopher was three he got him into the school. A friend told me about it.

CLH Did any official tell you?

Mrs Davis No, because he was under five and they don't take them under five really, so I was worried because to all intents and purposes he was an only child, and he had nobody to play with and he wouldn't mix with other children. I thought if he could be with other children it would be good for him.

Mrs Davis heard about the school from a friend, and got Christopher in via the doctor.

Mrs Richards, however, has had no help from official sources with regard to schooling.

Mrs Richards Jill is at home. There is nothing for her whatsoever. The only time she sees other children is Monday afternoons in the playgroup.

CLH How did you hear about that?

Mrs Richards Mrs Mercer advertises; and that's all she gets – two hours on Monday afternoon where she mixes with other children.

CLH How often does the health visitor come?

Mrs Richards She comes quite often from the clinic and is very nice. In fact she has been marvellous these last

140

couple of weeks. She has got on to them about Jill and no one else seems to have bothered about her at all. They put her into the hospital last year in a ward with twenty other children who couldn't speak at all. We discharged her after three days because I didn't think they could get a true assessment of her, not under those conditions, because she couldn't converse with any of the children. She ate with a knife and fork when she went in, when she came out she couldn't use them. The doctor was sympathetic but he still thought she would need a month in, but I don't know any other children who have been put in for a month. I have been trying since the beginning of September to find out what school she is going to after Christmas. After all if she was normal and I didn't put her name down I would be in trouble. Right? She is five now, she is due to be educated in some way and I have been trying since September but have got nowhere. I have had the health visitor get on to the education officer ... they always seem to pass you on to someone else and you get through to him and he doesn't know anything about it, so he passes you to somebody else and that's how it goes on, in a vicious circle. When you reach the end of your tether what help might you expect from the social services department?

Mrs Williams   I got on to the social services, I was crying me eyes out and I explained to them about what Bobby was doing – someone down the road had accused him of damaging his car – and they were more or less trying to put the blame on me, 'cos I was so upset, 'cos my husband was out of work. And she said to me, 'Have you any money problems?' and I said 'Well, no, we've got no money problems.' I said, 'It's just Bobby is my problem.' So I said, 'He just will not leave the van alone, and the man has been out, shouting at me, telling me about a twenty pound bill he'd be sending me if he does any damage.' So anyway I stopped crying, so she said to me,

'You feel better now you've explained it and got it off your chest.' And that was the end of that. It was a waste of two pence.

Mr Davis also feels that arrangements are made for him which he has not asked for or been consulted on and so are unsatisfactory.

Mr Davis You see I wouldn't dream of running a business and just making changes without getting my staff together and saying 'This is what we are going to do together and this is how it will affect you', and then you get people working with you; but this anticipation, what appears to be a void in communication, is bad. [Anticipation refers to the changeover of the responsibility for the school from the Health to the Education Department.] At a meeting of the parents' association with the chairman of the Health Committee I asked some pertinent questions: I said, 'If this is such an important meeting why is the local Medical Officer of Health not present?' and the chairman said 'I will answer the questions', and I rather took the line, 'Well I would like my questions answered by an expert' . . . What annoyed me was there was not another parent in the audience who got up and said 'Will you please answer the question Mr Davis has put?' I was absolutely on my own, so I shut up, because once I get my teeth into something then I like to see the conclusion. On the other hand, at a meeting like that with limited time, and they jolly well see it's limited time to answer questions, you don't like to hog the meeting because the rest of the audience will just react against you, but I would like to know what we are supposed to accomplish; it seems to be a dead end every time you get so far.

Mr Peters also said repeatedly during the interview 'They never tell you anything', 'You have to push all the time', 'They don't understand'. He felt that the authorities view him as a troublemaker and that he may not get what he is entitled to because he is always prepared to speak his mind.

The school is obviously the greatest help the parents receive. What is less satisfactory than the progress the school has achieved with the child, continues to be the quality of communication with the school. This problem must not be seen in isolation. Most schools and institutions do not find it easy to communicate with parents and outsiders. Nor can it be said, in fairness, that there is a complete absence of communication or that we have ever experienced great difficulties with the staff. Letters to the school are answered promptly and with great sympathy. Dates for closing, holidays and any administrative matters come to us on 'banda' sheets and that works well enough.

As we live more than five miles away from the school there cannot be the easy 'dropping in' that some of our best infant and junior schools encourage. There is the phone, but one doesn't like to bother anyone unless it is an urgent matter, in case the teacher is busy in her room. In any case not all parents have phones and not everyone talks comfortably on them.

There are parent afternoons and evenings: these are semiformal events when both sides are probably on their best behaviour. They ensure contact with some staff and are therefore to be welcomed; it is doubtful, however, whether staff have time to absorb information. What parents learn from these occasions is not certain. At best, parents will be completely satisfied by the meeting: to them it represents all that is wanted, and that is the impression I gained from two of the interviews. The best communication is achieved at our school from class meetings, where the teacher meets the parents in her classroom after lunch or after school hours and general discussion of problems can develop.

Evidence from 'normal' secondary schools suggests that this is not always the case. When parents meet teachers, both sides are likely to erect defences; the staff may be anxious: they can easily be much younger than the parents and they may feel less confident in their teaching techniques than they would care to admit to an outsider. Everyone who has taught knows this feeling of not having done enough. Furthermore, with mentally handicapped children progress, though often real, is slow and perhaps less apparent to those in constant contact with the children. Only today, when we went on an outing, did it strike us how much better behaved David was compared with a very similar occasion a year ago. So the teacher may feel that there is nothing to report, or that any indication of progress may be seized on by parents who are hungry for encouragement, which in the end will lead to nothing but disappointment.

As a professional group, teachers do not find it easy to talk to parents, perhaps for the same reasons that they do not find it easy to talk to each other about their work. They tend to be cut off from one another in the classroom, and talking shop is not always encouraged in the staffroom. This is particularly true of schools where staff relations are based on a strict hierarchy and junior staff are expected to be seen rather than heard. Asking for advice or discussing problems can be felt to be an admission of failure. One of the lessons many young teachers learn quickly is that it is best to keep oneself to oneself and to let others assume that there are no problems. Fortunately, this does not seem to be the case at our local school.

Parents bring their own difficulties into the situation: the very fact of having a mentally handicapped child is, for them, a failure. Whatever the inner feelings, when we face society most of us put on a brave front and the pain is hidden. The tradition of the stiff upper lip has its uses in war but I am more doubtful of its value when we are dealing with our children.

The parent–teacher association should be the place where experience and expertise can be shared. The degree of difficulty we experience in bringing up our handicapped children may vary, but the PTA should avoid at all costs setting up a kind of jolly club where there is so much activity that no one can be his true self. There should be a place somewhere where one does not have to pretend that all is well and that all our children need are annual outings and Christmas parties. Normal people, and sometimes even those who have mentally handicapped children, often seem to think the children are 'deprived', and a clear distinction must be made between 'deprived' and 'handicapped'. To other people who do not really understand what it is like to have a handicapped child we must become bores because we complain all the time. If the parent–teacher association is a place where genuine communication can take place, teachers have something of real value to give. They are more detached, have some professional expertise and can therefore help parents with bringing up the child they are both in contact with. One party can bring up the child without constant consultation with the other, but this seems uneconomical in experience and even in practical terms.

Consistency and continuity are important factors in all education; how, for example, can teachers and parents succeed in toilet-training unless they communicate with one another on the approach they have to the problem, what sanctions or encouragement they believe work and what words they use? We say 'pee' and school says 'toilet' and the child has to learn two words instead of one. This seems wasteful when one remembers that the mentally handicapped child has a limited vocabulary to work with in any case.

In all the work of the school the parents play a peripheral part and I wish we could change this. Surely a case conference without a parent present must be an extraordinarily one-sided affair. I am not claiming that parents should be allowed access to all information at all times; part of the expertise of the teacher must be to know what can safely be disclosed and what must be concealed. There is rarely agreement on this point: some patients want to be told when they are mortally ill; the majority of doctors think they would be better off without this knowledge. If the school had a clear idea of the parents' maturity and capacity to cope with information they would surely allow them greater participation? One of the problems in our society that we must learn to solve is the involvement of all in the running of the community to a greater extent than seems possible at the moment. In many of our institutions we who pay for them through our taxes and rates, who send our children to them, are completely excluded from the processes of consultation. With far too many of us, non-consultation has become a way of life, to the extent that it is neither expected nor demanded any more. Those of us who do want to participate are branded either as idealists or troublemakers.

Having a mentally handicapped child is bad enough, but what emerges from the interviews is that all the help which ought to be available has to be sought; this is easier for middle-class than for working-class people. Mr Gage explained to me what happened to him when his daughter Stephanie was sixteen:

CLH Do you get all the help you ought to have?

Mr Gage Well, I don't know, the thing is we don't get the attendance allowance any more. I think we lost it a few years back. Also Stephanie is now on supplementary benefit, and we have lost something in the region of five hundred pounds – you see when a child becomes sixteen you lose the family allowance because the child is supposed to start work. When she was sixteen the family allowance people sent a form asking, 'When is your son or daughter leaving school?' So I sent it back and said, 'Well, I'm very sorry but I don't know when she is leaving school.' So they said 'Carry on with your family allowance.' So that went on and then I get another form from the family allowance people for the same thing: 'When is your daughter leaving school?' So I went down to the Department of Health and Social Security and explained to the people there that she was mentally handicapped and I didn't really know when she was leaving school; so they said, 'All right, carry on with the family allowance.' Now at the adult training centre they wanted to explain to us what it was all about. So while I was over there I saw, I think it must have been one of the social services chaps, and I said to him, 'Can you tell me how long Stephanie will be at this adult training?' and he said, 'Well, no, we keep them there and work out what they can do and then transfer them to different places according to their ability.' I said, 'The only reason I am asking is because the family allowance people keep on asking when Stephanie is leaving school.' So he said, 'You shouldn't be getting family allowance.' I said, 'Well, I am sorry. I just don't know what is happening, then. I'm trying to be above board and say to the family allowance people I don't know when she is leaving and they say, "Just carry on".' Now he said, 'You should be getting supplementary benefit which is nine pounds a week.' That was the first time I'd heard of it and he said, 'If you go down to the DHSS they will give you a form and you could have it.' So I went down, yes, that was right, she was seventeen and a half and they said, 'Well, you know, no way we can give you the back pay, you've sort of lost that.' We worked it out – nearly eighteen months at nine pounds a week ...

Mr Gage had a competent social worker but it obviously was not enough in this Kafkaesque maze of social services. There are few villains in the tale, just muddle and lack of co-ordination and continuity. One of the ironies of the situation is that middle-class people think all the social services are busy on the housing estates.

Mr Strachey   I feel, too, that people who live on social security get quite a lot of help from the social workers, all the different things. It's different from us who earn our own living. They're known to the social security people because of all their problems. We're not. When you say they cannot help themselves, well, if they get a modern, forward-looking social worker, he would help them far more than he would you or me. He feels he's got to help them. It's not necessarily that we are a higher class but because we have a bit of knowledge. The social worker will think, 'Oh, they can look after themselves', and they will ignore our pleas for help more than they would for someone on those estates ...

I am afraid that Mr Strachey was as much caught up in the net of bureaucracy as Mr Gage. The only difference was that Mr Strachey had the confidence to persist and knew how to stir things up so that in the end Clive was found a place.

Mr Strachey   He was all fixed up to go to the training centre. Well, as we live in this part of the town we had a bit of a a fight to get him in. It was down the road, you see, nice and handy. Anyway, it was all fixed up and it was during the summer holiday, it went on and on and I didn't hear anything. A friend told us her daughter was going to the same centre, but not Clive. We left it for a few more days and then you rang the social worker.

Mrs Strachey   I had asked my friend, 'Where did you hear that?' and she said, 'From my social worker.' And I said, 'I come under the boundary here.' So I phoned the social worker. She knew nothing but she said she would inquire. She phoned back, 'There is no place for Clive at the training centre.' I said, 'Why not? He's been taken there and shown the place together with the other children from his school who are going; they wanted to prepare him.' And she said, 'There might be a place for him somewhere else.' So I thought, fair enough, and I prepared Clive, you know, you've got to prepare these sort of people for it or it just comes as a shock.

Mr Strachey   ... and then the social worker rang, there was no place for Clive; and Mary said, 'What are we going to do?' and she said, 'You will have to keep him at home.'

Mrs Strachey   I screamed down the telephone.

Mr Strachey   Mary rang me at work, I could tell she was terribly upset and I rang the social services, I don't know whom, I was so angry at the time. I would speak to a secretary and she would say, 'Oh, it's Mr So-and-so you want to speak to.' So I'd get back to the switchboard and ask for this Mr So-and-so. The secretary would again come on, his secretary, that is, and I would say, 'I want to speak to Mr So-and-so' and she would ask, 'What about?' Then she'd say, 'Oh, it's Mr Other-so-and-so you want', and I'd say, 'I've just spoken to *his* secretary and I was told to speak to *your* Mr So-and-so', and she would say, 'No, I'm sure that's not right.' So I had to go back again. I have heard of protective secretaries before, but this was just utterly ridiculous . . . in the end I got through to the head of the department and he said, 'There is nothing I can do.' I said, 'Yes there is. On the day that he is due to go to the training centre I shall be coming to your office and I shall be leaving Clive there and I'll come and get him at four. I'll bring him again the following day but that day I'll bring the Press with me; so you'll find somewhere for him, won't you?'

Mrs Strachey   They did.

Mr Strachey   He didn't like it, the fact he was beaten. 'Of course, you know,' he said, 'it'll harm him, the fact that you are going to have to take him away again.' They said they couldn't take him because there was no transport so I said, 'I'll take him, don't worry about the transport.' Of course as soon as they found they had to take him they organized the transport. If you can manage to get on top of them then you can beat them; it's no use asking. You've got to force them into it.

If one has a phone, a car and a forceful personality it still seems possible for people like Mr Strachey to get more out of the social services than the people from the housing estate! But it is such a shame that parents who already have so much to cope with in their own homes have to use up their remaining nervous energy on battles like this one. Since some local authorities have not yet compiled a register of the mentally handicapped, it is not known how many people have not been fitted into training centres or how many more places are needed.

COMMENTS AND RECOMMENDATIONS

1. Make sure your child is on the Register of the Mentally Handicapped which your local authority is required to maintain under the Chronically Sick and Disabled Persons Act, 1970. You are more likely to be informed of your rights if your name is on the register. The benefits may include the attendance allowance, family allowance, mobility allowance, family fund and in some cases vaccine damage payments. Addresses and details of how to apply are given on pages 162–6.

2. A member of the local authority social services department should visit the family and explain what help they are entitled to. This might be done in the form of a checklist; a number of authorities have issued pamphlets which list the kinds of help available. One snag is that if you are not on the register you do not get the pamphlet automatically, and if you are not informed of what is available you may not know what help you can get. There is some evidence that registers are not kept up to date (see *Handicapped Children; their homes and life-styles*, HDD Occasional Paper, 4/78, Department of the Environment).

3. If no one comes to see you, phone your local social services department or write a letter and keep a copy. The Department of Health and Social Security pays national pensions and the attendance allowance. Your social worker can help you to get the right forms and fill them in. You are entitled to these payments, they are in no way a charity. The Citizens' Advice Bureau or the secretary of your local association for the mentally handicapped may also be helpful and advise you.

4. Clear information should be given to the parents well before the child's fifth birthday as to what education he or she will receive if the child is not already attending a school or a special unit. It should not be left to the parents to try and find this sort of information for themselves. Every child has a legal right to some form of education from the age of five onwards.

5. Communication between parents and teachers could be improved. Too often they work with the same child but independently of one another. This will not help the child's progress and time and energy may be wasted in trying to teach the same thing in different ways. Parents should be encouraged to drop in at the school informally – perhaps to collect the child when this is feasible – and regular informal meetings between parents and teachers should be encouraged. When there are case conferences the parents should be able to attend.

   Parents may be told that schools are for teaching children and that their visit may disrupt the programme. This makes the boundaries between living and learning too rigid and defeats the aims of educating the mentally handicapped child. Parents may be told that there is no demand for communication: create the demand by asking for it. Try to get the school to help you draw up a programme for educating your child. Some common objectives may well be established and if there are behaviour problems you might join forces to tackle them constructively. Do not think that all schools and teachers take kindly to this sort of communication. Avoid attack and confrontation, but persuade and allow trust to develop.

   Some schools have started a diary for each child which passes between school and home. This makes sure that both sides know what they are doing. If the school tells you that the diary gets lost, that parents don't want it, that parents can't write and so forth, find a school where this system works. It can be done.

6. Make sure that there is a parents' representative on the school governors' board and that you are in touch with them. This is one of the things a parent–teacher association can do effectively. It should not just exist for fund-raising and entertainment.

7. If the child cannot start at the school till the age of five, some sort of playgroup or nursery class is essential.

10 THE FUTURE

All being well, we would like to die in ripe old age, knowing that our children are settled, happy and secure. When there is a mentally handicapped child in the family another dimension is added: if the child has survived into adulthood there is a good chance that he will outlive his parents. There is also the possibility that by then the family will no longer be united or one parent will already be dead. The rate of marriage breakdown and illness through stress is considerable. One thing is certain: when the parents die someone else will have to look after the child. We live from day to day and manage as best we can, but we are always fearful that there might be a crisis when we would not be able to support each other. Old age and incapacity come to be doubly dreaded. The mentally handicapped child, particularly if he has Down's Syndrome, is very likely to outlive his parents. This possibility must not be disregarded.

If money is no problem there may be private institutions. Some, like the Rudolf Steiner Association, have taught us how much can be achieved with mentally handicapped children and adults. If the child is fairly capable there may be a place on a Home Farm Trust establishment, but there are waiting-lists, stringent investigation before admission and, of course, the cost. If any establishment is well run and properly staffed the costs must be at least as high as those of a boarding school and parents should be very careful before they place their child in the care of any institution where the costs are low.

For the majority of children there will be no such choice;

there will be a place either in a subnormality hospital or in a hostel for the mentally handicapped. If there is no place, a great burden will be placed on the remainder of the family. I would certainly not expect my two sons to look after David. They have their own lives to lead, their own families to establish and it would be unfair to be burdened with their brother for years to come.

If society wants to look after the mentally handicapped it must share out the burden, even if this is the cost rather than immediate caring. It would be unrealistic to expect everyone to agree to do that. If the future means a place in a hospital or – increasingly, we hope – in a hostel, this adds other considerations to the problem of having a mentally handicapped child. All institutions inspire some degree of apprehension: the nineteenth-century buildings, and occasionally the severe attitudes of those times, are still with us. In recent years, thinking about placing the mentally handicapped in hospitals has changed. The most positive and encouraging ideas are expressed in Professor Mittler's report, *Helping Mentally Handicapped People in Hospital*, Department of Health and Social Security, 1978. The point is made that in 1978 50,000 citizens in the United Kingdom were living in hospitals for the mentally handicapped; of this number, 20,000 had lived in a hospital for twenty years or longer. It has become clear that of that large number, many do not need to be in a hospital: they are not sick, they do not need medical attention all the time any more than ordinary people do, and they can be helped to look after themselves much more effectively than used to be thought. It follows that alternatives for hospitals can and should be found. There could be minimum-support hostels and community schemes where groups of mentally handicapped could be supported. None of this sort of work can be left entirely to volunteers. There must be professional backing and advice and the sort of constancy that volunteers, with so many other commitments, cannot give even if their intentions are good and their energy and enthusiasm unlimited. Sadly, hostels for the mentally handicapped, like the ones for people discharged from mental hospitals or other institutions, are not always accepted in local communities. The tragi-comedy described at the beginning of the book is not as rare as it ought to be. There is a combination of ignorance and fear which has certainly been reduced but not eliminated. The National Association for the Mentally Handicapped, MIND, and the sympathetic approach of the media have all helped. There is goodwill when it comes to collections or jumble sales, but a home on the doorstep is quite another matter: first there is the confusion between mental handicap and mental illness. Invariably sexual assault and deviance are associated in people's minds and if, on top of that, there is the fear that the value of private property will suffer, the opposition can become formidable.

The Mittler Report states:

The conditions under which many hospital residents live are still far below the level that a civilized society should tolerate. We cannot afford the luxury of choosing between two priorities. We must develop community services because we believe that mentally handicapped people should be able to take their place in local communities as local citizens. But we must also do much more to ensure a better quality of life for those who are now in hospital and work to rehabilitate more hospital residents for a community which has previously had no place for them.

In past years hospitals for the mentally handicapped have not had a very good press: there were the scandals, and the publication of reports on the Whittingham and Ely Hospitals and, more recently, Normansfield. However, it is no use making scapegoats of some overworked and underpaid nurses, hospital administrators and doctors, or hoping that improvements will come because some punitive measures have made everyone feel that something positive has been done. Nevertheless, looking at hospitals after the inquiries it becomes clear that some good has come out of them. More constructive thinking about the mentally handicapped, their needs, how to look after them and how to improve their quality of life in hospital came after these stringent inquiries which were at last made public and not just hushed-up by a professional committee. The mentally handicapped and their parents do not make a powerful political lobby, they do not fill the postbags of their M.P.s with mail, and I fear that more dramatic and well-organized claims will take priority and so attract votes and funds. An excellent way to fob off a sectional interest is to point out that there are others equally miserable, equally deserving. I have felt guilty when told by a local authority official that it was rather selfish to press for hostel accommodation when there were so many homeless, deaf or arthritic people to be helped. A fair point, but I fear that these groups were in turn told about the urgent needs of the mentally handicapped. In any case I can speak for the one thing I personally know about and I have learnt that I must speak for the mentally handicapped because of David and the others like him who are so helpless.

Like making a will, we put off the evil day of doing something positive about the future because, just as the will reminds us of the inevitability of our death, so doing something positive about the future of a mentally handicapped adult is also a reminder of impending mortality, of the relative helplessness of the handicapped and of the need to look at hospitals or other alternatives. If we have to rely on hospitals we must accept what the area health authority offers. Ideally the future of the mentally handicapped must be planned with care. The needs of the whole family should be taken into consideration and as far as possible all concerned should be involved. If this is not done, when a sudden emergency occurs such as a serious illness or the death of one of the parents, the son or daughter may be rushed off to a hospital and the shock may make them helpless and depressed. As institutions have had a bad press some parents may hang on to their son or daughter for too long. The mentally handicapped mature in their own way; it may take longer but it happens. If they stay at home for too long they may become too dependent and too isolated. Certainly I have seen a development in David since he went away from home. As I have described, it was an upsetting experience but it must also be said that he was ready to be on his own.

even in the protected environment of the hospital. All children eventually leave home to set up their own families or lead independent lives. If they fail to do this, it may well be that part of their personality has not been allowed to grow, that parents have encouraged dependence and in some way derived a benefit from it. The move of the handicapped child away from the family should not only happen because it takes a great strain from the family (and the relief can be enormous); it should also be considered as an essential part of growing up.

Before the child is sixteen (that is the time when statutory schooling will no longer be provided) the future should be explored with the help of social worker, psychologist and teachers from the school who know the child well. The parents should be asked what they want and the alternatives should be presented clearly. We were asked to such an interview and we were impressed with the friendly and sympathetic way we were treated. I wished wryly that such a case conference had happened earlier, possibly when David started at school. However, what happened was sensible. Whether all parents could cope with such a large group of professionals, even though friendly and well-intentioned, I do not know, but on the whole it is better to be consulted than not and it is better to be made to think of the future than just to close our eyes and hope it will go away.

When faced with having to take one's child into a hospital it might be best to know what to look for. Hospital is associated with illness and going there may well be more frightening for the family of the handicapped person than the staff realize. After all, to them it is the place of work, where they and the patients may well be happy and contented, but to the outsider the unfamiliar may be alarming. If one is not an expert it is not easy to know what to look for or what makes a good hospital and which ones are not so good. Clues may be found in the way the newcomer and the family are received. Are questions answered openly, or are they avoided or referred to someone else? Are the rules and regulations easily understood and are they reasonable? Is the institution open and is visiting arranged to suit the convenience of the relatives or the staff? What is the daily timetable like? Does it meet the needs of the patients or the nurses? Can a patient go to bed for an afternoon nap when he feels like it or are there fixed bedtimes? Can the patients cook themselves a snack or make themselves a hot drink? Personal clothing is an important part of our individuality. Can patients wear their own things; can a choice of clothes be arranged; can they be kept in their own wardrobes? What are the laundry arrangements? Money is important: patients receive a disability pension and if they are able to understand the meaning of money they may well enjoy buying things. How are accounts kept and what is the money spent on? A great source of pleasure can be food and it is good if the weekly menu is displayed – one might ask if there are opportunities for choice. What is the dining-room like and how nearly like home is the setting for meals? Many attempts are made to reduce the size of wards, and where smaller rooms exist patients may be able to share a room with friends. It would be useful to know what is done to relieve boredom. This is not just a question of having the television set on but of what provision is made for occupational therapy, further education and entertainment, as well as for contact with the outside world. It is unfortunately the case that many of our subnormality hospitals are so far away from towns that visiting is not easy. Anything that is done to stimulate the patient, keep his or her interests alive and preserve contact with life outside must be encouraged.

Apart from skilled medical and nursing care, the following services should be available: speech therapy, occupational therapy, physiotherapy and dentistry. An optician's advice and that of an audiometrician should also be sought when necessary.

Probably it would not be wise or tactful to come to the hospital with demands for all these services at once. If parents know whom they can ask, where they can find explanations and voice their anxieties and possibly their fears, they will feel happier about leaving their son or daughter in the care of the hospital. More important, they should put as much pressure as they can on politicians and local authorities to make sure that provision for the mentally handicapped is of a reasonable standard. I am sure that the care we provide for the most helpless members of our society is a sure indication of the level of civilization we have achieved.

COMMENTS AND RECOMMENDATIONS

1. Come to terms with the fact that the future of the mentally handicapped child must be planned, and do something about planning the future before he or she is sixteen. Do not wait for a crisis when emergency measures might have to be taken: contact your G.P., your social worker or the head of the school if your child goes to a special school.

   Make sure your wishes and needs are known to the professionals. Your doctor, social worker, teachers or therapist are not necessarily in touch with one another.

   Accept the fact that your child, in order to mature, may need to lead a life without you. Sometimes the mentally handicapped are less dependent when away from their families and can do things their parents thought were quite beyond them. Find out what is available: is there an adult training centre and will there be a place for your child?

2. A decision to provide a future home by paying fees must depend on a place and on the means available. You should also consider the effect on the rest of the family. Is it sensible and worthwhile to opt out of a system for which you are already paying with your taxes? Consider also that the money you spend on one child may deprive others in your family. Will you be able to cope with the holidays, especially as you get older?

3. A hostel: will there be a place for your child? Will you be able to contribute and how much will that be? Will your child be at home during the holidays?

4. The subnormality hospital: what is it like? Contact the consultant through your G.P. The hospital provision may

be better than you thought. If it isn't, join one of the local pressure groups: the Campaign for the Mentally Handicapped, the National Association for the Mentally Handicapped, or MIND – they may be able to help and advise.

5. If your child is offered a place in hospital, look at the standards of provision. Locally, I found that a very useful pamphlet was published by the Community Health Council called 'Visiting Long-Stay Hospitals'. This was based on a text written by J. R. Elliott, *Living in Hospitals*. Your local Community Health Council may have similar information available. The national address is given on p. 164; you will be able to find out where your own Community Health Council can be reached. If you have any complaints or difficulties contact them.

   If you are not sure what standards to look for in hospitals for the mentally handicapped, look at the pamphlet *Helping Mentally Handicapped People in Hospital*, Department of Health and Social Security, 1978. It is an admirable and humane document and will set standards for years to come. Some hospitals offer good basic care standards but don't do enough to occupy and train patients. This booklet will help you to ask the right questions.

6. Be reasonable in your demands: don't offend or frighten the staff with a long list. They may have been fighting for better conditions for their patients for years and may be suffering from the economies imposed on them. It would be useful, though, to find out the issues on which the staff would welcome support, what to ask for and whom to approach.

Research has shown that too many people do not receive the help they are entitled to. With the information given in this book you may be able to help another family with a mentally handicapped child.

BASIC FINANCIAL RIGHTS

Attendance Allowance

This is a sum of money paid weekly to those whose circumstances fulfil the conditions which the National Insurance Commissioners have laid down:

A person has to be so severely disabled, either physically or mentally, that he requires, and has required for six months, from another person

1. *by day* (a) frequent attention throughout the day in connection with his bodily functions, (b) continual supervision throughout the day in order to avoid substantial danger to himself or others.
2. *by night* (a) prolonged or repeated attention during the night in connection with his bodily functions, (b) continual supervision throughout the night in order to avoid substantial damage to himself or others.

There are two rates of allowance, a higher rate payable for persons meeting the day- *and* night-time conditions, or a lower rate for those who meet the day- *or* night-time conditions.

There are complications which need to be looked at closely:

1. If you have applied for the higher rate and been refused there is nothing to prevent application for the lower rate.
2. Once the application has been made, the DHSS arranges for an examination, usually by the applicant's own doctor, who fills in a form. It is important that the questions are answered *fully*. For example: you may just

say 'yes' to the question, 'Can he get into the bath?' The fact that a handicapped person cannot bath himself without assistance must be mentioned.

3. The form is forwarded to a doctor appointed by the Attendance Allowance Board. He decides whether or not to award the benefit. If this is refused the claimant has the right to apply for a review within three months. Ask for a review; a large number of people are awarded the allowance after review.

4. The letter applying for a review should give as many details as possible and the claimant should state clearly why he thinks he is entitled to the allowance. For example, mention the danger the handicapped person faces if left unattended – give instances of previous falls or accidents.

5. Good reasons must be given for the decision to refuse to grant the allowance. If the Review Officer does not do this it may constitute an error in law which can lead to the matter being referred to a Commissioner by the parent or his/her representative.

The attendance allowance is worth having: it is not taxed and does not debar you from getting supplementary benefit or family income supplement. You may have to persist to get the allowance. Get someone to help you with the application, for instance, a social security officer, your social worker, a member of your local group for the mentally handicapped or a parent who has already obtained the allowance. To apply for the attendance allowance, complete form DS2C (for a child) or DS2 (for an adult). The forms are available from the local offices of the Department of Health and Social Security. Tell your doctor that you are making an application.

Mobility Allowance

A new allowance for handicapped people who are judged medically 'unable to walk or virtually unable to walk'. The allowance is to be spent on outdoor mobility and can be used in any way – on a car or on taxi fares, or to pay for holiday transport, etc. Ask for leaflet NI 211 from your social security office. In making the application you may need the same sort of help and support as for the attendance allowance.

Non-contributory invalidity pension

The pension is for people over sixteen 'who do not qualify for sickness or invalidity benefit because they have not got enough national insurance contributions'. Ask for leaflet NI 210 – other benefits are listed on the back of the leaflet. It is advisable to start applying for this well before the child's sixteenth birthday. He has to have an insurance number first and then a letter from the doctor.

Vaccine Damage

In May 1979 a scheme was introduced to provide lump-sum payments for persons who have been severely damaged by vaccination for the following diseases: diphtheria, tetanus, whooping cough, poliomyelitis, measles, rubella (German measles), tuberculosis and smallpox. For further information, ask your G.P. or social worker, or write to the Vaccine Damage Payment Unit, Department of Health and Social Security, North Fylde Central Offices, Norcross, Blackpool FY5 3TA.

Tax relief. Ask your Tax Inspector.

How to get what you are entitled to

If you are not receiving the right allowances or the support you need, or if you have a complaint, find out what the most effective channels are. Community Health Councils are now widely established. Your own Area Health Authority will give you the local address or you can write to the Association of Community Health Councils for England and Wales, 362 Euston Road, London NW1 3BL. The secretary may well be able to advise you on how to make an approach and where it should be made. Check that you are making representations to the right authority: is it a money or a tax matter, an educational provision, or something to do with health? These all involve making separate approaches to different authorities. Many local authorities have produced pamphlets which explain what you are entitled to if you have a mentally handicapped child. Some of the more active societies have produced their own pamphlets (for example, *Mental Handicap – a Review of Services in Bristol and District*, Bristol Campaign for the Mentally Handicapped. The fourth edition of this excellent pamphlet has just been published. Write to: 6 Alfred Road, Windmill Hill, Bristol 3 (50p per copy).

When dealing with government and local authorities be prepared to be patiently persistent. It is an advantage to own a telephone. If you have to phone social service departments or the Department of Health and Social Security from a coin box, take a large number of coins with you. You may well be shunted from one department to the next and it takes time. Always make a note of the name of the person you are talking to, the details of the call, the date and the time. When you have to make a complaint it helps to have a detailed list of names, times and promises made.

Remember that officials are not necessarily your enemy. They may have sympathy for you but they are not always able to help and in some authorities it seems to be the policy not to volunteer information. You get what you ask for, but they do not come to you with suggestions.

Join an action group which is prepared to make a noise on your behalf.

Start early to apply for a place in a Steiner-type village, Home Farm Trust or a group home, but be realistic – there are not enough places and it may cost a lot. A subnormality hospital may be a solution and many family tensions may be resolved if your child can be admitted. Hospitals may not be perfect but many have improved during the past few years. The improvements will continue if parents make themselves heard.

165

Group homes and minimum-support hostels, professionally supported and adequately staffed, would be the best solution for a large number of the mentally handicapped. They are not sick but their condition is a permanent one. They need help to be able to help themselves.

USEFUL PUBLICATIONS

BOOKS

ADAMS, M., *Mental Retardation and its Social Dimensions*, Columbia, 1971. Studies by the Child Welfare League of America.

BULL, D., *Family Poverty*, Duckworth, 1967.

CARR, J., *Helping your Handicapped Child*, Penguin, 1980. A step-by-step guide to everyday problems.
Young Children with Down's Syndrome, Butterworth, 1975.

CHRISTOPHER, E., *Sexuality and Birth Control in Social and Community Work*, Temple Smith, 1980.

COOPER, E. and HENDERSON, R., *Something Wrong?*, Arrow Books, 1974.

COUSINS, J., *Make it Happy*, Penguin, 1980. An excellent, down-to-earth approach to sex. Not really intended for the mentally handicapped. It has a comprehensive list of addresses for help needed with sexual problems.

CRAFT, M. and A., *Sex and the Mentally Handicapped*, Routledge, 1978.

FURNEAUX, B., *The Special Child*, Penguin, 1973 (revised edition in press). This ranges over the whole field of special education and is written with authority and sympathy. There is a good bibliography.

GOFFMAN, E., *Stigma*, Penguin, 1968. Discusses the idea of a 'spoilt identity' and describes the defences one puts up against the outside world. It taught me a great deal about myself and my defences when 'stigmatized' by having a mentally handicapped child.

GREENGROSS, W., *Entitled to Love*, Malaby Press, 1976.

HALE, GLORIA (ed.), *The Source Book for the Disabled*, Paddington Press, 1979.

KEMP, R. and C., *Child Abuse*, Fontana, 1978.

KEW, S., *Handicap and Family Crisis*, Pitman, 1975.

KIRMAN, B. H., *The Mentally Handicapped Child*, Nelson, 1972.

KURTZ, R. A., *Social Aspects of Mental Retardation*, Lexington Books, 1977.

LONSDALE, G., ELFER, P., and BALLARD, R., *Grief and Social Work*, Blackwell, 1979. Describes the feelings of parents when presented with terrible news about their children. A constructive approach on how to deal with painful emotions. Mainly for professionals.

167

MCCORMACK, M., *A Mentally Handicapped Child in the Family*, Constable, 1978.

MCNAMARA, J. and N., *The Special Child Handbook*, Hawthorn, 1977. Written for use in the United States. It is very comprehensive and covers many handicaps. Shows what community initiative can be taken.

MANDELSTAM, D., *Incontinence*, Heinemann Health Books, 1977. A guide to the management and understanding of a very common complaint.

MITTLER, P., *People not Patients*, Methuen, 1979.

NEWSON, J. and E., *Patterns of Infant Care*, Penguin, 1965.
Four Years Old in an Urban Community, Penguin, 1970.
Two useful books on the changing patterns of child-rearing.

OSWIN, M., *The Empty Hours*, Allen Lane, 1971.
Holes in the Welfare Net, Bedford Square Press, 1978.
Children Living in Long-Stay Hospitals, Heinemann Medical Books, 1979.

PARFIT, J., *Services for the Young Handicapped Child*, National Children's Bureau, 1972. An overview of provisions made in various parts of the country. It may be a source of ideas if parents want to suggest projects to local authorities. (Address, p. 171)

PATERSON, B., *Help!*, Peacock Books, 1977. Nothing to do with mental handicap as such but a useful guide to adolescent problems.

STAFFORD CLARK, D., *Psychiatry for Students*, Allen & Unwin, 1974. This shows how limited and reactionary the outlook towards the mentally handicapped can be. For a sharp and critical reaction see Newsletter No. 14, Campaign for the Mentally Handicapped, 12 Park Crescent, London W1N 4 EQ.

STONE, J., and TAYLOR, F., *A Handbook for Parents with a Handicapped Child*, Arrow, 1977. Invaluable for addresses, ideas and names of societies.

WARNOCK, M., *Meeting Special Educational Needs*, HMSO, 1978. A brief guide to the Report of the Committee of Enquiry into the Education of Handicapped Children and Young People. An important and stimulating document.

I would like to stress that this bibliography is in no way exhaustive or the last word on the problems related to mental handicap. I hope that some of the books will be a useful introduction and there are fuller bibliographies in many of them.

PAMPHLETS AND ARTICLES

ADRIAN, HESTER, *Parental Involvement Project*, University of Manchester, 1976.

BRINKWORTH, R., and COLLINS, J., *Improving Your Mongol Baby*, NSMHC. Contains a useful list of other publications and mentions the important help and advice developed by Rex Brinkworth. Obtainable (like their other publications) from the NSMHC Bookshop, 117–123 Golden Lane, London EC1Y 0RT (01-253 9433).

Useful Publications

CLARKE, A. D. B. and A. M., *Practical Help for Parents of Retarded Children*, Hull Society for Mentally Handicapped Children, 1969.

COSSEY, D., *Safe Sex for Teenagers*, Brook Advisory Centres, 1978.

Department of Health and Social Security, National Development Group for the Mentally Handicapped:

1. *Planning Together*, 1976
2. *Children. A plan for action*, 1977
3. *Helping Mentally Handicapped School Leavers*, 1977
4. *Residential Short-Term Care*, 1977
5. *Day Services for Mentally Handicapped Adults*, 1977

Creating a Learning Environment (Chapters 5 and 6 of a Report to the DHSS, *Helping Mentally Handicapped People in Hospital*, 1978, reprinted as a pamphlet with excellent bibliography).
All pamphlets available free from the DHSS, Alexander Fleming House, Elephant and Castle, London SE1 6BY.

Department of the Environment, *Handicapped Children: their homes and life-styles*, HDD Occasional Paper 4/78. An important piece of research which shows how badly parents fare, particularly mothers, the importance of keeping registers and what helpful provisions can be made.

JACKSON, C., *They Say My Child Is Backward*, NSMHC.

The Jay Report 1979. An inquiry into mental handicap, nursing and care – consultation and comments were invited by the DHSS. Full Report or summary obtainable from HMSO, or inquire at your library.

Kith and Kids, *One to One*, obtainable from Maurice Collins, 6 Grosvenor Road, London N10. A report about a project of working with handicapped children on a one-to-one basis of child and volunteer.

Parents Information Bulletin No. 13, *Mental Handicap A–Z*, NSMHC. Some of your questions answered – the addresses of regional welfare secretaries are given and the questions most often asked are given practical answers. It will be invaluable to people working with the mentally handicapped and their parents.

Patients First. A consultative paper on the structure and management of the NHS. HMSO, 1979.

SHEPPERSON, B., 'Attending to Need', *New Society*, vol. 24. A study of thirty-seven families with mongol children: are they getting the attendance allowance? Which are the families that are not receiving it?

SOLLY, K., *The Different Boy*, NSMHC.

STONE, J. and TAYLOR, F., *Camden Handbook for Parents with a Handicapped Child*, Department of Social Services, Camden, 1974.

USEFUL ADDRESSES

Afasic Association (Association For All Speech Impaired Children), 347 Central Market, Smithfield, London EC1A 9NH (01–236 3632)
   (Concerned with children and young people whose primary handicap is a language disorder)

Association for Spina Bifida and Hydrocephalus, Tavistock House North, Tavistock Square, London WC1H 9HJ (01–388 1382)

Association of Parents of Vaccine-Damaged Children, 2 Church Street, Shipston-on-Stour, Warwickshire

Breakthrough Trust, 66–8 Greenwich South Street, London SE10 8UN (01–691 6229)
   (A group helping deaf adults and children)

British Epilepsy Association, Crowthorne House, New Wokingham Road, Wokingham, Berkshire RG11 3AY (0344 63122)

British Psychological Society, St Andrew House, 48 Princess Road East, Leicester LE1 7DR (0533 549568)

Brook Advisory Clinic, 233 Tottenham Court Road, London W1 (01–580 2991)

Campaign for the Mentally Handicapped, 12 Park Crescent, London W1N 4EQ (01–636 5020)
   (A pressure group for mentally handicapped people – pamphlets, conferences and research)

Concord Films Council Ltd, Nacton, Ipswich, Suffolk IP10 0JZ
   (A non-profit-making body and the best source of films about mental handicap)

Disability Alliance, 5 Netherhall Gardens, London NW3 (01–794 1536)
   (A group that campaigns for the rights of all disabled people; provides an advice service)

Useful Addresses

Disabled Living Foundation, 346 Kensington High Street, London W14 (01–602 2491)

Down's Children Association, Quinborne Community Centre, Ridgeacre Road, Quinton, Birmingham B32 2TW (021–427 1374). Also many local Associations
(Advice and support centre for parents with mongol children)

Elfrida Rathbone Committee, Tom Blythe Centre, 34 Islington Park Street, London N1 (01–359 7443/4)
(A social work agency, operating in Islington and Camden, with an under-5 unit, hostel for teenagers, recreation for adults, literacy unit and sheltered housing – all for E.S.N. (M))

Family Planning Association, 27 Mortimer Street, London W1 (01–636 7866)

Home Farm Trust, General Manager, 57 Queens Square, Bristol, Avon (0272 292060 and 294359)

'In Touch', Anne Worthington, 10 Norman Road, Sale, Cheshire
(Correspondence magazines to put parents in touch with other families of mentally handicapped children)

Invalid Children's Aid Association, 126 Buckingham Palace Road, London SW1W 9SB (01–730 9891)

King's Fund Centre, 126 Albert Street, London NW1 7NF (01–267 6111)
(Publish a catalogue of clothing for the handicapped and disabled)

Kith and Kids, 6 Grosvenor Road, London N10 (01–883 8762)
(A society based in North London. Provides playgroups, etc., for local children, information and counselling)

MIND (National Association for Mental Health), 22 Harley Street, London W1N 2ED (01–637 0741)

(MIND Exchange is an advice and information service. It supplies pamphlets and information sheets, addresses and advice, e.g. on where to get genetic counselling if it is unobtainable locally)

Monteagle Centre for Brain Damaged Children, 151 Station Road, Knowle, Solihull, West Midlands B93 0PT (056 45 77982)

Muscular Dystrophy Group of Great Britain, Natrass House, 35 Macaulay Road, London SW4 (01–720 8055)

National Association for Deaf/Blind and Rubella Children, 61 Sennelys Park Road, Northfield, Birmingham 31 (021 475 1392)

National Campaign for the Young Chronic Sick, 94 Marlborough Flats, Whitton Street, London SW3

National Children's Bureau, 8 Wakley Street, Islington, London EC1V 7QE (01–278 9441)
(Information and advice centre)

National Society for Autistic Children, 1a Golders Green Road, London NW11 8EA (01–458 4375)

National Society for Brain-Damaged Children, 35 Larchmere Drive, Hall Green, Birmingham 28 (021 777 4284)

National Society for Mentally Handicapped Children (MENCAP), 117–123 Golden Lane, London EC1Y 0RT (01–253 9433)
(Publishes a quarterly magazine, *Parents' Voice*)

National Society for Phenylketonuria and Allied Disorders, 26 Towngate Grove, Mirfield, West Yorkshire (Chairman: 0603 54811)

'New Prospect', Roy Hull (editor), 23 Primrose Croft, Hall Green, Birmingham 28

NFER Publishing Co., Darville House, 2 Oxford Road East, Windsor Berkshire
(Supplies materials for the Portage Project, a home-based training scheme for developmentally delayed pre-school children)

Post Help, Dave Watkin, 42 White Farm Road, Four Oaks, Sutton Coldfield, West Midlands
(Parents' pressure group for better facilities for over-sixteens)

Pre-School Playgroups Association, Alford House, Aveline Street, London SE11 (01–582 8871)

Riding for the Disabled Association, National Agricultural Centre, Kenilworth, Warwickshire (0203 56107)

Royal Association in Aid of the Deaf and Dumb, 7 Armstrong Road, London W3 (01–743 6187)

Rudolf Steiner Association, (Head Office) Rudolf Steiner House, 35 Park Road, London NW1 6XT (01–723 4400); Camphill Rudolf Steiner Schools and Village Communities: Camphill Rudolf Steiner Schools Ltd, (Central Office) Murtle House, Bielside, Aberdeen AB1 9EP (0224 47935)

The Spastics Society, 12 Park Crescent, London W1N 4EQ (01–636 5020)
(Advice, assessment, residential care, job training)

Toy Libraries Association, Toynbee Hall, Commercial Road, London E1
(Central address for libraries all over the country which lend toys and give advice on play with handicapped children)

Voluntary Council for Handicapped Children, 8 Wakley Street, London EC1V 7QE (01–278 9441)
(Advice and information on all handicaps)

INDEX